ABOUT
WAR

ISBN printed book: 978-1-83952-378-6
ISBN e-book: 978-1-83952-379-3

Cover design by Kevin Rylands
Internal design by Andrew Easton

Printed and bound in the UK

This book is printed on FSC certified paper

ABOUT
WAR
Making Sense of War

Christopher K Pike

BROWN
DOG
BOOKS

To the memory of

Cpl Clifford Pike RAF, served 1940 to 1946,
UK and Burma

'I did my bit'

ABOUT WAR
ACKNOWLEDGEMENTS

Many people have inspired, helped and facilitated this book; too many to mention all individually.

I have consulted an enormous number of sources, including unpublished academic dissertations, books, articles, Wikipedia (to get dates right) and a huge number of informative and authoritative websites.

Special thanks must go to the academic staff at King's College London War Studies Department who put structure and insight into my concept of strategy and the political aspects of war.

Cornerstones Literary Consultancy offered timely facilitation and reassurance. Ed Handyside of Myrmidon Books provided encouragement and his percipient comments transformed a series of monographs into a coherent book.

Frances Prior–Reeves, my project editor, took a sensible business-like approach to the challenge of transforming a manuscript into a book, and that was complemented by Etty Payne of Elegant Words who did a tremendous job of proofreading.

Nicky Bird of Bird Battlefield Tours had an eagle eye for excess verbiage and historical references and Lawrence Wragg provided a cool assessment of structure and format. Professor Dr Paul Cornish of Coracle Analysis and the Chief Strategist at Cityforum encouraged and supported me along the long path between draft and publication.

Most of all, Christine Salter, my partner, was tireless in her encouragement and support, as well as a keen eye for proofreading and research, structural comments and also, never to be forgotten, coffee at the appropriate time!

As is usual, all errors, emissions and inaccuracies are mine.

'War is only a cowardly escape from the
problems of peace.'

Thomas Mann

'I hate war as only a soldier who has lived it can, only
as one who has seen its brutality, its futility,
its stupidity.'

Dwight D. Eisenhower

'Battle is the most magnificent competition in which a
human being can indulge. It brings out all that is best;
it removes all that is base.'

William Tecumseh Sherman

'I have never advocated war except as a
means of peace.'

Ulysses S. Grant

Carl Philipp Gottfried von Clausewitz (1780 to 1831) Prussian staff officer and military theorist, and, later in life, the director of the Kriegsakademie, the Prussian Staff College

Clausewitz's famous dictum that 'war is a continuation of politics by other means' is a misinterpretation of what he actually said (as explained in the text). He also suggested a 'trinitarian' approach to war, which encompassed *passion* – which he attributed largely to the people (he hated the French); *logic* – which he attributed largely to the government and *chance* – a domain of the military.

Coincidentally, this 'Trinitarian' approach echoes Thucydides' *'fear, interest and honour'*. Clausewitz thought of war as a way of achieving political ascendancy over an enemy. He gave little thought to the enemy or what their objectives might be. War was regarded differently before Napoleon, so commentators now talk of the 'Napoleonic Clausewitzian' paradigm.

A modern approach might be that whilst recognising Thucydides' and Clausewitz's dicta, and as we have to live with whatever enemy we identify, *victory* should be accompanied by *peace* (see text) and, as peace is of limited utility without it, *justice.*

There are thus three 'trinities' when talking about war: Thucydides', Clausewitz's and 'victory, peace and justice'.

Clausewitz is one of the relatively small number of great military thinkers, such as Machiavelli, Howard and Freedman, but was he in his time and of his time.

INTRODUCTION

This is a book about war: what it means, how it's directed and what role it might have in the future. War has been ubiquitous ever since man walked upright and has been instrumental in the rise and fall of great empires, the creation of great art, architecture and literature, and technological and managerial innovation. History is concerned with diplomacy, politics, religion, and economic and social changes but it is war, an uncertain business, that has caused an unimaginable number of deaths, massive destruction and, repeatedly, the end of what was once thought of as the established international order.

John Donne said famously that 'no man is an island, entire of itself' and, similarly, no nation state or other polity is an island politically; each exists and operates in an international system, with rules and norms built up over centuries. This book examines the international context for war and, as examples, some of the attempts to control and moderate war.

Such attempts involve *strategy*, one of the most misused words, much to the detriment of the understanding and execution of the whole concept. Strategy is the link between both international and domestic politics and war itself and whose meaning now needs to be expanded to include any and every other hostile action taken by one state or polity against another. War is a political act, and every action taken should be oriented towards achieving peace and a better political balance between protagonists.

But the relationship between politicians and the military is an uncomfortable one and, in some cases, breaks down entirely – witness military coups. The relationship between civilian and military leaders is not generally given the attention it needs, much to the detriment of both the political and military agenda.

It might be thought that, in future, technology will run wars, but politics and war are intensely human activities and thus, although technology will have a strong influence on war, it will not determine it.

Nuclear weapons cast a dark shadow over international politics and war, with nuclear Armageddon being a perennial nightmare. The risks seemed to lessen following the end of the Cold War in 1990 but may now be increasing. Constant effort should go into minimising the risks of nuclear war. We should strive to keep the nuclear non-proliferation concept alive and the extension of New START (Strategic Arms Reduction Talks), which was due to expire in February 2021 is to be welcomed. The Americans, under Trump, had been disinclined to address this: Biden has taken it more seriously. Even so, perhaps it is time for Europe, with two nuclear-armed states, to distance itself from US foreign policy. This book examines several writers with military experience who imagine a nuclear war being limited to just one weapon on each side, the calculus of a political balance being paramount.

War is not comprehensively understood, sometimes impatiently initiated and, often, through weaknesses in strategic control, simply unsuccessful. Some political scientists suggest, perhaps optimistically, that fewer than half of all wars achieve their original objectives for those initiating it. Consider Korea, Suez or Vietnam or, more recently, Afghanistan, Iraq and Libya. Regardless of faction, the war in Syria has been murderous, tragic and without purpose to the vast majority of the population.

How do we think about war? How do we put meaning, direction and purpose into a coherent framework?

This book explores these issues in straightforward, practical terms and posits that contemporary procedures and processes for the governance of the nation state at war within the Western model of liberal, democratic government are simply inadequate to the task of planning for and executing future war.

It discusses war in general as a political act and draws examples from the UK's experience and governance of wars.

CONTENTS

1. WAR IN HISTORY: |
THE PERSISTENCE OF WAR

War has no origin. Historians can trace the provenance of all other social activities like trade, democracy and indeed civilisation itself; it is 'mankind's greatest experiment', according to archaeologist Richard Miles, but war defies such easy analysis. War holds a unique place; no other social activity purposefully organises men, women and matériel to kill and destroy. War is phenomenally expensive, both in terms of the accounted costs (lives lost and property destroyed) and the opportunity costs (resources that might have been used to improve the lives of citizens being diverted to preparing for or prosecuting war). At the height of the Soviet regime in Russia, some 27% of its GDP was spent on defence. There are also less obvious social psychological costs, from individuals suffering from post-traumatic stress disorder and debilitating physical injuries through to a damaging exultation of the winning side and resentment from the losers.

AN HISTORICAL PERSPECTIVE

War has been a constant theme and backbeat for all groups, clans and civilisations. It used to be thought that primitive societies, such as Upper Palaeolithic and Neolithic peoples, indulged only in ritualistic warfare – standoffs between groups with few casualties and a one or two deaths, perhaps of weaker, unlamented members. Archaeological and paleoarchaeological (archaeology with bones) evidence now suggest that not only did ancient groups wage war on other groups for territory, slaves, resources or women, but that the encounters could be expensive in terms of deaths and injury. War accelerated after the first agricultural revolution around 10,000 BC and indeed gave the migrant and itinerant

Early battles, although modest in size, were probably very nasty. If you survived an initial wound, infection would probably kill you

groups an attractive rationale for attacks on the new settlements. War was a constant theme thereafter, the first cities providing a clear focus for the attacking side to plunder. Jericho, for example, was reckoned to have been in existence from around 8,000 BC until Joshua 'fit the battle' and 'the walls came tumbling down' about 1,400 BC. Archaeological evidence shows that Jericho's walls had substantial foundations, suggesting strong, defensive walls, even in around 8,000 BC.

The first empires were committed to expansion, by attacking other territories for the usual prizes of plunder, slaves, artefacts and access to natural resources. Security played a part, a concept we will deal with later.

Save for archaeological evidence, little is known about early battles and the first recorded was the Battle of Megiddo, fought in 1457 BC between the Egyptians under Pharaoh Thutmose III and a rebellious coalition of Canaanites led by the King of Kadesh, now in modern Syria. War continued throughout the classical period. The Greek city-states thought of the summer as the season for war and generally had a go at ... well, anyone, but mainly other Greek city-states. Only rarely did they come together to fight a common enemy.

The Romans were almost permanently at war. During the Republic, Principate and Empire they could always find someone to serve as an enemy, largely to establish their individual and collective *virtus* and of course to gather slaves and plunder. War was almost constant throughout the Dark Age and with the violent spread of Islam. There was no let-up during the Crusades, the 12th-century Renaissance, the Mongol invasions (1206 to 1405), the 14th-century (Italian) Renaissance, the Reformation, Counter-Reformation or various other religious conflicts.

The end of the Thirty Years' War, during which everybody had a go at ... well, everybody else was marked by the institution of the Westphalian state system in 1648. This established the idea, still current today, that each state had exclusive sovereignty over its own territory. (This is covered fully in Chapter 4.) Wars still continued apace, an outcome of the Westphalian system simply being that there was more clarity about who was actually fighting whom. One might have hoped that the Enlightenment, the Age of Reason, would provide a more rational approach to war, but there was no such luck; the Enlightenment coincided with a thirst for empire and, of course, no Briton could let North America or India fall to the French (or vice versa), and so wars continued apace. The Industrial Revolution served to industrialise war, causing even more deaths, destruction and an institutionalisation of the whole practice.

There were occasional periods of relative peace during this time. The second century from Trajan to Commodus was relatively peaceful in Rome itself (after the internecine bloodletting of earlier times), but most Roman emperors were involved in various wars around the Empire. Even the Black Death, with fewer people to fight, did not lessen war's impact. According to Wikipedia, the first half of the fourteenth century recorded seventy battles; the second half, seventy-three. Historians have coined the term the long peace for the period following the end of World War II in 1945, but this is rather rose-tinted judgement rooted merely in there having been no hot war between the five members of the United Nations Security Council: the USA, the Soviet Union / Russian Federation, China, the UK and France. There were a sufficient number of proxy wars to make up the numbers.

Looking at the UK alone, British forces have been in action every year in one theatre or another from 1945 to the present day, during which time there have been over 7,000 operational deaths.

CURRENT WARS

At the time of writing, the Syrian civil war may be in its concluding stages, but how many other ongoing wars are there? There are several sources of information, but rather than delving into each one, we can quote Wikipedia for a general overview. Wikipedia divides wars into three categories. First are those with more than 10,000 deaths in the past year (major wars), of which there are three: Afghanistan, Syria and Yemen. Wikipedia's next group is wars with between 1,000 and 10,000 deaths in the past year, these include Somalia, Iraq, Boko Haram in Nigeria and Cameroon, South Sudan and Mali. Then there are twenty-five conflicts with fewer than 1,000 deaths in the past year. Excluding the 'Mexican drug war' (13,300 deaths in the past year) and the 'Philippine drug war' (886 deaths in the past year), there are fifty-six ongoing wars

The Roman Army was tough, well trained and with fierce discipline but their success came equally from their excellent logistical and supply arrangements

worldwide, with 110,000 deaths in the past year and a cumulative death toll of over 4.6 million since those wars started – some as far back as 1947.

Of course, the quantity number of wars and their appalling carnage is only one part of the problem. According to the UNHCR (United Nations High Commission for Refugees), as of 2017, over sixty-five million people (about the population of the United Kingdom) have been forcibly displaced worldwide because of persecution, conflict, violence, or human rights violations. Of these, twenty-one million are displaced from their country of birth, forty-one million are Internally Displaced Persons and over three million are asylum seekers. For reference and since they involve armed soldiers, the UN has currently fourteen Peace Support Operations around the world.

Many of these wars appear to be intra-state or civil wars rather than inter-state, yet in many cases other states are involved. We are familiar with the United States-led coalition invasion of Afghanistan, Iraq and Libya (which was actually only bombed), but consider the war in Syria. Countries involved include the United States, Russia, Turkey, a putative Kurdistan state and the non-state of ISIS. The war in Yemen is supported on one side by Saudi Arabia and on the other, allegedly, by Iran. Other countries cannot avoid culpability either, since comparatively little attention is given to the states who supply the arms. The biggest arms exporters in the world are the United States, Russia, China, France, Germany, the United Kingdom, Spain, Italy, Ukraine and Israel, with combined military exports amounting to nearly $120 billion, depending how this is measured. Some of the backers of one side in a civil war are also those who supply the arms to the other.

Time, then, has not served to temper war, neither has any form of social organisation nor any international treaty nor intergovernmental body. Mankind has experienced every conceivable form of government with every form of group, tribe, clan, culture, nation, state or polity. Any list would be lengthy. RationalWiki lists forty-one forms of government, from *Anarchy* to *Tyranny*. This applies to every size and geographic location of state, nation or polity. Despite the assumption that ideology is a key driver of war, there's little evidence to support it. The Western assumption that liberal, free market democracy is the answer to almost any problem has yet to be proven.

Yes, there are now more constraints on war, but, if the past is anything to go on (and what else do we have?), wars will continue.

2. WHAT IS WAR?

War will mean different things to different people. For the grandparent generation, *the war* meant the titanic struggle with fascism that culminated in the Second World War, 1939 to 1945. For the next generation, that of baby-boomers, the war, and although they did not experience it directly, was referred to frequently by the then parents; the austerity, bombsites and rationing (certainly in the UK) were constant reminders. Subsequent generations have had only limited exposure to war: it is something that happens somewhere else; it is about guns, bombs, death and destruction – but someone else's. But to many people in other countries, war – or at least physical violence – is a constant threat. Many countries have not seen an absence of war – or peace – since their colonial masters left. The Democratic Republic of Congo is a tragic example.

What exactly is war? There are a few agreed definitions and even then, most of them miss its essence, which is that war is a political act. The guns, bombs, death and destruction are a means to an end, not ends in themselves. Given the considerable cost to both sides in waging war, in terms of what the Americans call 'blood and treasure', one might expect that *war* would have a very precise meaning. One would be disappointed. Defining war is not as straightforward as might be imagined.

CONSTITUTIONAL DEFINITIONS OF WAR

The United Nations was set up formally in 1945 (the term had been used during the war to designate the Allies), *to save succeeding generations from the scourge of war, which twice in our lifetime has brought untold sorrow to mankind.* The UN's purpose was *to maintain international peace and security*, etc. (from the preamble to the UN Charter, 1945). Yet the organisation gave no specific definition of *war* as such. It does have a reasonably cogent description of *aggression* as opposed to war, citing, for example, *invasion of a state by the armed forces of another state … port blockade* etc., but it admits that even arriving at this was tortuous. The UN Charter forbids war, so states' military actions are more often described by states as 'emergencies', 'self-defence', 'policing actions' or even as 'humanitarian interventions'. There is little about politics, domestic or international.

The United Kingdom Constitution, being largely undocumented, has no guidance on the subject and no definition of war. The US Constitution has little guidance either. There are more words devoted to the issue of copyrights and patents in the US Constitution than any definition of Congress's role in declaring war. The US Department of Defense has a 400-page book entitled *DOD Dictionary of Military and Associated Terms* (*Acceptability* to *Working Group*) but it does not contain any definition of war as such. One might have thought a definition appropriate for such a department. Despite a few half-hearted attempts, it is not until we get to the French definition that politics gets a look in: *War is defined as a state of armed conflict between several constituted political groups, such as states. States wage war against other states, not individuals or their families. Thus, war is defined as an act of foreign policy or defence of last resort after final negotiations of diplomacy.*

War has been around for ever, but can we put the War of the Spanish Succession of 1701 to 1714 (around 300,000 casualties) into the same category as the Football War, fought between El Salvador and Honduras in 1969 (maybe 3,000 casualties) or as existential wars, such as Nazi Germany versus Soviet Russia, which involved such horrendous carnage on the Eastern Front (more than 14 million military deaths and 20 million civilian deaths)?

The original Constitution of the United States, 1787. The famous words 'We the People' established the concept of government 'of the people, by the people for the people'. Many other countries worldwide might follow the same concept

THE NEED TO DEFINE WAR

War must not be conflated with *warfare*. *War* is a political act in the realm of politicians and diplomats. It is the realm of strategy and social considerations. *Warfare*, on the other hand, is the practice of conducting the war on the battlefield or war-space. It is the realm of soldiers, sailors and airmen, of munitions, logistics and geography and, increasingly, cyber-warriors. The enemy is there to be beaten, or at least persuaded to conform to the victor's will. All this may seem rather obvious or even banal, but ponder the considerable media coverage of most wars: pictures of ruined cities – think of Syria – or arguments about defence budgets or analysis of the capabilities of the latest aircraft carrier. Politics, the relationship between different polities, is taken as implied or even ignored. Examples of this abound, but a few will suffice to illustrate.

It is well known that the Americans' knowledge of Vietnam before the eponymous war of 1955–1975 was scanty. Anyone with any knowledge of Libya before the bombing in 2011 would have been well aware that tribal divisions were only kept under control by the dictator, Muammar Gaddafi, and that removing him would inevitably result in the carnage that followed. NATO might also have anticipated that the transition from dictatorship to a modern democracy might take years.

And yet the money and resources spent on political intelligence and deliberations before those wars is overshadowed by the fantastic cost of even just one of the new F-35 fighters that the RAF and Fleet Air Arm say they 'really need'. War is a political act but it is often reported as warfare. Peace movements, too, often focus on the horrors of war – no, *warfare* – rather than the political effort.

Then comes the difficulty of assessing and understanding *change* in both war *and* warfare. Most of the reported changes in *war* are actually changes in *warfare*. Though we are fortunate in the United Kingdom to have a wealth of influential commentators on war, the distinction between *war* and *warfare* is elided in much of their output.

There is also a legal dimension. The laws of war are part of international law, agreed by almost all nation states. These govern particularly the treatment of prisoners of war and civilians. Next, we must distinguish between *war* and *crime*. One lone person, or a very small group, attacking a government building and causing casualties, would be classed as a criminal offence, notwithstanding their assertion that their motives were 'political'. But suppose they were reacting to a state's brutal oppression (at the time of writing, Sudan or Syria would be a good example of this): might their actions then be considered to be war?

A WORKING DEFINITION OF WAR

However, if we change the perspective, stepping back from the immediate, we can see that almost all wars are about the relationship between different polities. A *polity* is a group of people with a collective identity with the capability of collective effort, the best example being the nation state. War is about politics, both internal, to rationalise the interests of the group, and external, relationships with other polities or states.

WAR DEFINED

War is a hostile act of coercion or the threat or use of organised violence designed to change the political balance between polities.
A polity is a social organisation which is coherent and largely supported by its members.
Such a polity must be capable of providing security and other social goods, such as governance and justice. The obvious example is the nation state.

An important concept is that of *changing the political balance*. Many definitions of war assume that 'victory' is the end of the matter, but unless a defeated enemy is completely destroyed, as the Romans did to Carthage in 146 BC (except for those people they could sell into slavery), or as Hitler wanted to do in Russia between 1941 and 1943 (excepting those people they could use as slaves), victory represents only part of the balance. That balance must recognise that the two previously combative states have to live with each other in the post-war world. Although France suffered terribly at the hands of the Germans in both world wars, both countries are now closely aligned and allied in the European Union.

Another key concept is the ability to run a state. We say *state* here, but this could well include federated areas or an authority such as in Palestine. For military action to qualify as war, that polity must be capable of assuming the responsibilities of governing a state. Some

In June 1625, the Dutch governor of Breda surrendered the keys of that city to Ambrogio Spinola, the Genoese general commanding the Spanish 'tercios'. Immortalised in a painting by Velázquez, 'The Surrender of Breda' (1635)

examples of varying degrees of the ability or lack of it follow.

- The Confederacy in the American Civil War was perfectly capable of assuming the responsibilities of the nation state, despite being in rebellion.
- Al Qaeda's objectives, which included a worldwide caliphate,

were unrealistic, and they were not capable of governing a state.

- The FLN (Front de Libération Nationale) in Algeria were politically mature while they struggled with what they saw as their French colonial masters. The political maturity was in the form of having a coherent Cabinet, an ability for collective effort and a very clear consensus on their ultimate goal: independence from France. They assumed full governmental responsibilities after the French had left.
- Even such a romantic figure as Che Guevara recognised that his idea of *foco*, a rolling revolution gathering strength through the peasantry, was not enough to take over the state: 'It is well established that guerrilla warfare constitutes one of the phases of war; this phase cannot, on its own, lead to victory ...'.

There is simply too much focus on warfare and not enough on war as a political act. Pause and think about all the war films one might have seen. With very few exceptions, most are about the soldiers, machinery, location and big bangs. Few address the political aspects of the particular war. One source of the *Top 100 Best War Movies*, for example, gets down to Number 26, *Lincoln*, released in 2012, starring Daniel Day-Lewis and directed by Steven Spielberg, before there is any consideration of the politics. The next is at Number 56, *Judgment at Nuremberg*, a 1961 film starring Spencer Tracy and directed by Stanley Kramer.

WARFARE DEFINED

Warfare is the practice of planning for, managing and using organised violence, be that military force or any overt hostile action (such as a cyber-attack).

It has many dimensions: doctrine, 'operational art', tactics, but it is essentially subordinate to the (political) essence of war ...

War is, therefore, a tricky concept and, unless our politicians and thus the military are absolutely clear about the distinction between war and warfare, we are doomed to repeat the same mistakes as we saw in World War I, Suez, Vietnam, Afghanistan, Iraq and Libya. Some might even add Korea and any number of wars, civil or otherwise, in Africa.

In 2013, David Miliband gave a speech at Ditchley Park. He recounted how he attended Cabinet in 2005–2006 as a minister. During discussions on the impending deployment of British troops to Afghanistan, he recalled arguments about money, equipment, drugs and governance. But not mentioned was the main point – politics not troops. That is, the politics of 40,000 villages and valleys, of a society where the state has no monopoly on violence, of complex tribal structures that cross national boundaries one hundred years after their creation; warfare as logistics, not politics.

Commodore Steve Jermy was deployed to Afghanistan in 2007. In his book, *Strategy for Action*, he recalls spending time in Whitehall beforehand. At no stage, he claims, was there ever a group meeting with the Ministry of Defence, Foreign and Colonial Office, Department for International Development and the Home Office to identify and define a clear political objective and to articulate a strategy for the deployment. Upon arriving in Afghanistan, he asked his staff what the plan was. The response was immediate: 'No idea sir, we're just getting on with it.'

A major theme of this book is that politicians who invoke war should be very clear about their war aims and about how military force will be converted into political gain, the link being strategy, of which more in Chapter 6. Politicians – and here they should be guided by the military – should also be very clear about what sort of war is being fought. The war in Afghanistan morphed from a counter-terrorist campaign, to defeating the Taliban, to a counter-insurgency campaign (and, by the way, let's eradicate poppy growing) to state-building and improving the lot of women, to some unrealistic notions of 'freedom and democracy'. It's small wonder that the only success in Afghanistan was down to the Taliban who fought a brilliant counter-insurgency campaign (NATO being the insurgents) clothed in pyjamas and shod in flip-flops (as the NATO powers saw it), using hundred-year-old rifles that the British had kindly left them the last time they were there, plus, of course, the munitions provided to them by the US during the Soviet counter-insurgency campaign of 1979 to 1989.

CATEGORISING WAR

Many commentators attempt to classify war in an attempt to render it more understandable and hence manageable. But they are largely talking about *warfare*. There is 'low intensity', 'high intensity', 'total war', 'inter-state war', 'intra-state war' (civil war) and any number of combinations. The US military even have an acronym, MOOTW (Military Operations Other Than War). It is less used now, but was defined as operations designed for 'deterring war, resolving conflict, promoting peace, and supporting civil authorities in response to domestic crises'. The UK military has crafted an equivalent term, *Peace Support Operations*, which might include peacekeeping and humanitarian support.

OTHER HOSTILE ACTS: WAR OR WARFARE?

It cannot be repeated enough: war is a political act, the realm of politicians and diplomats; warfare, on the other hand, is the practice of conducting war on the battlefield or war-space.

Let us end with a quotation from Sir Michael Howard, the doyen of military historians and founder of King's College London War Studies Department. 'Let us ... consider war as a great socio-political activity, distinguished from all other activities by the reciprocal and legitimised use of purposeful violence to attain political objectives ...'. Even he, one of the greatest thinkers on war in the twentieth century, does not distinguish sufficiently between war and warfare.

3. CAUSES OF WAR; CAUSES OF PEACE

The question of what causes wars fascinated people throughout the nineteenth and twentieth centuries. Prior to the Napoleonic Wars of 1792 to 1815, few thought of war as particularly unusual. Summer was the time for campaigning, though the troops had to be home in time for the harvest. Professional armies (and most were) might winter wherever they happened to be if it was too far to return home. The aristocracy would use winter for hunting as a substitute for war and to keep themselves and their horses in good condition for the next summer campaigning period.

Answers to the question: *what causes wars?* are elusive. There seem to be three main approaches: first, looking to the last war as guidance for the next; second, aggregating all previous wars on an empirical basis, trying to link these to the historical record and drawing conclusions; third, a political science approach involving models of political ideology, geopolitics, internal dynamics and any other seemingly relevant factors. Let us examine each of these approaches and seek some indications.

Following the first approach, understanding of previous wars, well grounded or not, has always played a powerful role in preparing for the next crisis and indeed the future conflict. Some thought that if Germany stayed unified after the Second World War rather than being partitioned into West Germany and East Germany, it would wish to create another German Empire. It is now well known that Margaret Thatcher (UK Prime Minister 1979 to 1990) had great reservations about the reunification of Germany in 1990. At one famous seminar in Chequers, she naïvely accepted that the Germans were 'untrustworthy'. Politics is about how different groups of people negotiate the relationship between themselves: root causes, agreed and disputed, need to be identified and resolved, not consigned to a dustbin marked 'politics'. This applies not only to the political side but is also interrelated to the physical preparations for war. As quoted in the *Oxford Handbook of War*, Georges-Henri Soutou makes the point that: '… war, history and the objectives of war are intrinsically linked …'. He suggests that France, in 1940 was '… wonderfully prepared for the last war …' (viz World War I). The Blitzkrieg defeat of France by Germany in May 1940 bore this out.

The second approach involves aggregating previous wars on an empirical basis and trying to draw conclusions. No one would disagree that any observation would need to be put into the historical context. Here, though, we come across a remarkable observation by the late Sir Michael Howard. In his invaluable *The Causes of War*, he starts by saying that: 'No one can describe the topic that I have chosen to discuss as a neglected or understudied one …'. He goes on to say: 'How many scholars from how many specialities have applied their expertise to this intractable problem! Mathematicians, meteorologists, sociologists, anthropologists, geographers, physicists, political scientists, philosophers, theologians and lawyers are only the most obvious of the categories that come to mind …'. But then he makes a remarkable assertion: 'Yet it is not a problem that has aroused a great deal of interest in the historical profession … but the phenomenon of war as a continuing activity within human society is one that as a profession we take very much for granted.'

Indeed, how many history books have somewhere within their pages the classic phrase: *war broke out*. But war does not simply break out; somebody breaks it out. War is about human agency, not random happenings. If one reads only a few books on military history, one cannot but think of what these particular troops (ships, planes) were doing in that part of the world, at that time, and what they wanted to achieve. Many military histories may only offer a perfunctory account of the political environment and situation that pertained. Few historians or military historians manage to integrate both factors. A good example of this might be accounts of the December 1941 attack by the Japanese fleet on Pearl Harbor, Hawaii. It is comparatively rare for accounts of the attack to admit that United States sanctions on Japan were crippling her economic growth. This is not to say that Japan had a legitimate reason for attacking the United States, but the motive needs to be recognised. Although it was a tactically brilliant move for the Japanese, in strategic terms it was a complete and utter disaster for that country.

Each war is unique in terms of its causes, its progress and its outcome. War is a political act, with the objective of achieving a better political balance between protagonists. The motives for most wars – on either side – are complex, and not subject to any one particular factor. Both sides need to accept that a war will be fought. Efforts to discern an overall answer to the question *what are the causes of war?* may well be worthy but, no less than any other aspect of history, evidence needs to be considered very carefully. Yes, there are lessons that we can identify; the problem is applying them.

The third approach, using quantitative models and empirical observations, is the realm of political scientists. A full analysis is beyond the scope of this book, but a few observations are useful. The concept is known as *multi-variate analysis.* Quantifiable variables such as population, GDP per head, the Gini coefficient (which represents the income distribution within a country) and other variables are incorporated into a model with – and here may be the snag – *quantified* empirical evidence. The problem is that the more variables you have, the more unreliable the answer. It would not surprise anyone that a country with enormous differences in income might be more susceptible to civil war. Political science models are useful as a guide, a starting point, but they often fail to address the core question.

'ACCIDENTAL' OR 'SILLY' WARS

Some wars simply defy any logical analysis as to causes. Although some may be triggered by accidents or misunderstandings and some for absurd reasons, there is often an underlying cause, however obscure. Also, we need to differentiate between the underlying cause of courses of the war, and what occasioned it.

Some examples; The War of Jenkins' Ear (1739), The Spanish–American War (1898) The War of the Stray Dog (1925) and The Football War (1969) are detailed in the chapter addendum.

OTHER FACTORS

There are two other factors which, if not the causes of war, certainly contribute to it. Geopolitics is easily appreciated, the political leaders who invoke war perhaps less so.

GEOPOLITICS

Geopolitics is the study of the impact of the Earth's physical geography – climate, topography and natural resources – on the relationship between polities, be they nation states or sub-national geopolitical entities (such as a federated state within a federal system). As such these polities might include different ethnic groupings and concern those ethnic groupings' access to some of the natural resources. Tim Marshall's *Prisoners of Geography* is a classic on this subject. Geopolitics is somewhat overlooked now, but retains a powerful influence on inter-polity relations. The most obvious example is water supply. Upstream users of water can extract more water and thereby disadvantage or even punish users further downstream. This has already been a problem between Pakistan and India, Sudan and Egypt, Israel and Palestine, and some of these conflicts remain unresolved. No doubt these could be addressed peacefully, but our interest here in this book is about war: what it means, how it is directed and what role it might have in the future. Geopolitics may not be the sole determinant of why individual polities go to war with others but it is absolutely crucial to understand the historical background to any individual state or polity.

A word here about the difference between Great Britain and other states. In the United Kingdom, it may be more difficult to understand other states, other than those with a similar geographic. Great Britain is surrounded by sea, and 'dangerous waters' (as defined by Dr Sam Willis, a naval historian) and therefore any invader has to negotiate, at the very least, twenty miles of open water. In fact, the last violation of British territory was the Battle of Fishguard in South Wales in 1797, where French forces were quickly repulsed by local militias. One of the great admirals of that era was John Jervis, 1st Earl of St Vincent, and he is famous for saying in the House of Lords: 'I do not say that the French cannot come, I only say that they cannot come by sea.'

The best and most proximate example of geopolitics is Russia, be that Soviet Russia (pre-1991) or the Russian Federation that succeeded it. Russia, however constituted, is generally portrayed in the West as antagonistic, truculent and led by a small clique of kleptomaniac ex-KGB thugs. This may be partly true, and we might also recognise that Russia has played its hand badly over the past thirty years (though that may also be true of the West). Various attempts by statesmen over the past few years, the latest being President Emmanuel Macron of France, to 'reset' the relationship have not been successful. But we need to understand why Russia is so sensitive regarding its relationships with other states. For a start, it is the largest country in the world. Russia covers 17,000,000 km^2, almost twice the area of China and twice that of the USA. This means it is inherently vulnerable to attack from almost any quarter. In terms of its relationship with Western Europe, we need to examine its history. Tim Marshall points out that Russia has been invaded many times from the west. Prior to the Napoleonic Wars, both the Poles and the Swedes attacked Russia over the North European plain. Here we have the perfect example of geopolitics: there are very few physical barriers between northern continental Europe and western Russia. Among other things, Napoleon is famous for his invasion of Russia in 1812, where 'General Winter' (another geopolitical fact of life) disposed of his army in very short order, not to mention his own egregious hubris. If we include the Crimean War of 1853–1856 and the two world wars up to 1945, the Russians were fighting on average in and around the North European plain once every thirty-three years. Furthermore, and despite assurances to the contrary, NATO now extends right the way up to the Russian border. Small wonder that Russia is sensitive in this regard.

LEADERS

Many wars and campaigns are inextricably linked with famous or infamous leaders. Would the Romans have conquered Gaul without Gaius Julius Caesar? Probably, but not in the way that Caesar did it between 58 and 50 BC. Would anyone but Charlemagne have established the enormous Frankish Kingdom in the 8th and early 9th centuries? Probably not. The whole thing fell apart in civil wars in the years after Charlemagne died.

Genghis Khan, Emperor of the Mongol Empire (the largest contiguous geographic empire ever), was a murderous thug. Unfortunately for his victims, he was also a very competent military leader. He conquered most of Eurasia, often massacring hundreds of thousands of civilians. His legacy has now faded, but he adopted the Uyghur script, established meritocracy and religious tolerance, unified the nomadic tribes of northeast Asia and brought the Silk Road under one cohesive political

Genghis Khan was one of the world's most murderous thugs, something that could equally apply to Hitler and Stalin. He is credited with wiping out between 10 million and 80 million people in the Asian steppe, Mongolia, China and also some of Eastern Europe. Unfortunately for his victims, he was highly intelligent and an outstanding general

environment, bringing easier trade between northeast Asia, Muslim southwest Asia and Christian Europe.

After its revolution, Republican France wanted to expand its franchise but not to the extent of Napoleon's personal megalomaniacal ambition. Hardly anybody today talks of the 'Wars of 1793 to 1815', they are always known as the 'Napoleonic Wars'. Strangely, given the French death toll for Napoleon's wars ('I can lose 30,000 French lives a month,' was his proud boast), he is still honoured in France today.

Then, of course, the ultimate question is whether we would have suffered the Second World War without Hitler and, correspondingly, would the Allies have prevailed without Churchill, Roosevelt and Stalin. There is little consensus on this, but one might guess that, even without Hitler, Germany would again have lashed out, but probably satisfied itself with the Sudeten Czechoslovakia, Poland to the east and Alsace -Lorraine to the west. Of Churchill, Alanbrooke, Chief of the General Staff, famously said that 'we would have been lost without Churchill'. He also famously said that 'he didn't know what to do with him but that he didn't know what to do without him'. From such a brilliant general, this is praise indeed. Of course, we often forget that the Second World War was won with American and British matériel and Russian lives.

A comparatively recent example, and one that still resonates in the United Kingdom today, is the British, French and Israeli débacle at Suez in 1956. This had more to do with Prime Minister Sir Anthony Eden's personal antipathy towards Gamal Abdel Nasser (the feeling was mutual) than anything to do with the Suez Canal. Eden probably thought Nasser an 'uppity colonial' (a nasty term, though current in those days) and wanted him dead. He saw him as a new Hitler, though Nasser was a smart Nationalist Egyptian rather than having megalomaniacal intentions. And, if politics is the art of the possible, was it really credible that Egypt would acquiesce to British rule (again), or even to Britain having a major influence in Egyptian affairs, as they had before the Second World War? History can always find leaders, great or otherwise, who have instigated and prosecuted war sometimes to great effect, often simply leaving a trail of death and destruction behind them.

SUEZ

In 1956, Nasser, the Egyptian president, nationalised the canal, much to the annoyance of the British Prime Minister, Sir Anthony Eden. Together with French and Israeli troops, British forces invaded Egypt to recover the canal. The American president, Eisenhower, was incensed and threatened a run on the pound. Britain backed down and withdrew her troops. Egypt kept the canal.

Suez damaged UK/US relations but these recovered. For the British, it was a watershed moment and many commentators have observed that it was the end of Britain's imperial preoccupations and that from then on, indeed to this present day, the British would, more or less, follow the US lead on foreign affairs.

For a more complete description of Suez, see the addendum at the end of this chapter.

Stepping back then, we can identify four main themes on the causes of war, but first we might record what one soldier from ancient Greece said.

Like all Greek citizens (not everybody was), Thucydides fought the Peloponnesian war (431 to 404 BC) and wrote the classic 'History of the Peloponnesian War'. He is attributed with commenting that what caused the Peloponnese War was 'Spartan fear of Athenian power'. He also diagnosed the cause of war as 'fear, interest and honour', an axiom difficult to beat.

THUCYDIDES ...

... was an Athenian soldier who fought in the Peloponnesian War between Sparta and Athens from 431 to 404 BC. He was also an historian, and his major work, *The History of the Peloponnesian War*, is the classic account of that conflict. It may seem strange to dig him up after two and a half thousand years, but he made two interesting comments that, eerily, still resonate today. He said that war was about 'fear, interest and honour': *fear* that you might be attacked (the security dilemma); *interest* in another polity's natural resources or their trade connections; *honour* as the standing of your polity in relation to others. Greek city-states thought of the summer as the season for war and most years had a go at any and every other city-state. Only rarely did they come together to fight a common enemy – Salamis (480 BC) and Plataea (479 BC) being notable exceptions when they beat off the Persian threat – fairly permanently as it transpired. Thucydides also described the motives for the Spartans in going to war with the Athenians simply: 'The growth of the power of Athens, and the alarm which this inspired in Lacedaemon (Sparta), made war inevitable.'

FOUR MAIN THEMES ON THE CAUSES OF WAR

It is intriguing how Thucydides' words echo down the ages. Stepping back or adopting 'helicopter vision' is always challenging, but looking at the evidence in front of us from Sir Michael Howard, Georges-Henri Soutou, Tim Marshall and countless political scientists, we can identify four main themes that indicate the causes of war.

The first theme is the anarchic nature of the International System. *Anarchy*, in our context (which is discussed briefly below), is the belief that there is no higher power for resolving international disputes. Each individual state has a 'legitimate monopoly of violence', which is the German philosopher Max Weber's (1864–1920) definition of a state. Whereas a breakaway polity may also achieve a legitimate monopoly of violence, that does not in itself make it a state *per se*. Of course, this then becomes a moot point: if the established state is judged oppressive or murderous, then the breakaway polity may be recognised as a legitimate state and thereby have acquired the legitimate monopoly of violence. Although the United Nations can, through various resolutions in the General Assembly or in the Security Council, encourage and even cajole various states to desist from their hostilities, the UN has no absolute power to do so. Unlike the state, the UN has no armed forces at its disposal and so each member state must take care of its own security and survival.

The second theme is *ideology*. The Cold War, from 1947 to 1991, was a stand-off between the United States, supported more or less voluntarily by much of the Western world, and the Soviet Union (1922 to 1991), which coerced much of Eastern Europe into following and supporting it. At issue was the liberal, capitalist, free market democracy of the West versus the communist version of socialism of Soviet Russia. Fortunately, the two main protagonists did not descend to a hot war (bang bang) but there were many proxy wars with each party backing different sides of

RATIONALITY AND WAR: JAPAN'S DECISION FOR WAR IN 1941

In December 1941, Japanese seaborne fighters attacked the US Pacific Fleet Headquarters at Pearl Harbor. It was a surprise attack on a neutral country at that time. Japan intended the attack as a preventive strike to keep the United States from taking military actions against them in Southeast Asia. Instead, it woke a sleeping giant. The attack was brilliant tactically but a strategic disaster. It brought the United States into the war in both the Pacific and Europe Hitler declared war on the United States four days later. It condemned Japan to nearly four years of suffering and over five million deaths. The war culminated in the devastation of the atomic bombs dropped on Hiroshima and Nagasaki in August 1945.

There is no common standard for rationality. For Hitler it was rational to invade Russia, for Lebensraum (living space). We might disagree.

Churchill's decision to fight on after Dunkirk has been called 'Irrational stubbornness'. But with America in the war, Churchill was delighted. He couldn't lose; the gamble of 1940 had paid off.

For a more complete description of Pearl Harbor, see the addendum at the end of this chapter.

conflicts all over the world. Portrayed generally as an ideological war between 'freedom and democracy' and 'guided but fair' ideologies, in fact the contest had probably less to do with ideology and more to do with the straightforward struggle for power and geopolitics (Europe providing the Geo bit). The Soviet Union encouraged communist parties in various countries around the world to do what they could to further the cause of communism, up to and including armed revolt. However, many of these communist uprisings were in fact little more than ways of settling existing disputes, or wars of ascendancy for particular revolutionary leaders.

The third theme is *security* and what is known as the *Security Dilemma*. *Security* is such a well-used and hackneyed term for which we in the West tend to forget its true meaning. Any sailor will be familiar with the concept that if the boat is not secure then neither is any crew member. Similarly, if the state is not secure, then neither is any citizen. In its most basic sense, security is *physical* security, in that if the individual is attacked then one has a remedy through the Police Force. Likewise, if the country is attacked, then we have the Armed Forces to defend us.

The Security Dilemma is where one state builds up its military strength, or makes alliances with other states (such as NATO) for what they claim are defensive purposes. Another, possibly neighbouring, state might see such alliances not as defence measures but as preparations for aggression and so might be obliged – partly from expediency, partly through pressure from its electorate – to build up its own military strength. This might continue until each now heavily armed state feels it needs to use its military strength to resolve a dispute that might otherwise be resolved peacefully. Some realist academics suggest that the security dilemma is actually the most important source of conflict in an anarchic world system. They assume security is the principal motive of states, and insecurity the major cause of war.

The fourth theme is *standing*, or *honour*. This is suggested by Richard Ned Lebow, a Professor of International Political Theory, who, has studied inter-state wars since 1648 (the Westphalia treaty). He proposes, and this may contrast with much of international relations theory, that wars are not fought primarily for reasons of security but for standing, honour or even revenge. Standing might be read as prestige or respect, or even influence. From a realist perspective, this might sound gratuitous, but consider one of the many causes of war in the twentieth century. Certainly, one (but only one) of the motivations for Germany to go to war in 1914 was Britain's reluctance to allow them to have a navy of similar size. Germany thought it deserved an Empire along the lines of the British and would therefore need a navy of comparative size to the Royal Navy. The British disagreed. Similarly, before the Second World War, the Japanese felt that they did not have the respect from the United States that they deserved. This culminated in the United States restricting Japanese access to oil and other natural resources, leading ultimately to Pearl Harbor. There were also racist overtones: the Americans thought of the Japanese as an 'inferior race', mirrored somewhat by the Japanese attitude to the Chinese.

The late Sir Michael Howard suggested that honour, seen as standing or self-respect, has always played a great part in war. He suggests, for example, that had a peace treaty been arranged in the middle of the First World War, at a point where there had been no clear victory for either side, then it would have been seen to betray and thus dishonour those who had already sacrificed their lives.

A similar problem affects current relationships with both Russia and Iran today. Both great nations in their time, they feel they do not get the respect that they deserve from the international community and particularly from the US or the UK. More recently, the standing of the United States may have been damaged by the Trump presidency, and if the country slowly fades in importance, it will feel the lack of respect and honour acutely. We can only hope that this does not encourage them to lash out militarily. And, given their difficulties in coping with a post-imperialist world, even the British (or maybe just the Conservative Party) might just feel the same.

PEACE AND SECURITY

As we have seen, the causes of war are complex and interrelated and dependent on any number of other factors, including accidents. Considerable effort should thus go into defining war, the causes of war and how we might prevent war. Let us also recall the aphorism, variously attributed: 'if all you've got is a hammer, all problems look like a nail.'

Relatively less effort goes into defining peace, the causes of peace and how the international community supports and develops peace. One extraordinary thing about the modern world is that if you are involved in reporting on or and advising on war, making armaments or prosecuting war, then there is an enormous amount of money to be made. It is difficult to get an idea of the worth of the global arms trade, but the Stockholm International Peace Research Institute estimates that the total value of global arms sales in 2017 (the latest figures available) was at least $95 billion and that the top one hundred arms companies made an estimated $398.2 billion worth of sales in that year. The US accounted for thirty-six per cent of world military spending in 2018. However, if an individual wants to pursue peace, they are condemned to a life of relative poverty. Although working for an NGO might provide a reasonable salary, that NGO has to raise funds – beg for donations (most NGOs are charities) to stay operational.

Peace is also difficult to define. In the United Kingdom, memories of *The War* (the Second World War) have almost completely faded. Peace is now the norm. Few would recall the deprivations of the years between 1939 and 1954 (the year rationing ended), the bombing and the bomb shelters, and the enormous effort put into war production. In parallel, the United States did not have to endure bombing or rationing (there was some, but very little) and their incredible gearing up of their industrial base for wartime production provided a launchpad for their subsequent economic growth. But even then, people in war-torn countries – such as

On Sunday 7 December 1941, Japanese carrier-based aircraft attacked the US Pacific base at Pearl Harbor on O'ahu in the Hawaii Group. Dubbed 'a date which will live in infamy' by President Roosevelt, it brought the United States into the Second World War, ended American isolationism and set the US on the path to globalism. With America's almost unlimited industrial might, she could fight on two fronts and not lose. Churchill was delighted. He could not lose either. The purchase of the Spanish territories in 1803 (the Louisiana Purchase) and the purchase of Alaska (1867), established the United States as one of the great nations of the Earth

some central African states – would not appreciate peace in the same way as would most people in the Western world. For although they might have enjoyed periods during which there was an absence of war, they may not have experienced the security the Western world enjoys. In short, peace, or even the absence of war is of limited value without security. Peace then, is much more than the absence of war; war is much more than the absence of peace. The linking dimension is *security*, which, in the context of war, largely means physical security – freedom from harm or other coercion. Furthermore, there are many subcategories of security and the whole concept has spawned numerous university and think-tank departments focusing on almost anything to do with security. *Security Studies* is now a popular subject. A couple of examples will illustrate the more general concept. These are essentially *subjective* securities, those that avoid problems rather than providing solutions.

Health security is where the population feel secure in the knowledge that the government of the day will be able to handle social health issues such as the provision of clean water and the prevention of pandemics or epidemics or the provision of healthcare in the event of major natural disasters. Much of the population in Europe would also add diagnosis and treatment of health issues, something not readily available in the US.

Financial security, which does not mean that everybody is assured of being rich, is the knowledge that the money transmission and investment services offered within the country are secure and that deposits and savings are reliably protected in some way.

Social and political security, which does not necessarily mean a welfare state, is being free to express your own opinions, and being able to advocate with impunity political views that are not generally held.

A full account might mention energy security, food security, natural resource security. (Lithium, for example, is only mined in certain countries, yet is vital for manufacturing some electronic components.) Academics seeking research funds may also have the word *security* tagged onto their application to encourage funding.

'LEAVE US ALONE.'

Some years ago, a journalist recently returned from Pakistan gave a talk at King's College War Studies Department. He had been in FATA (the Federally Administered Tribal Areas) in Pakistan and had outlined some of the insurgency/counter-insurgency that had been going on there, and the problems that Pakistan had had in these areas.

At the end of his excellent and detailed talk, he was asked a question. After offering thanks, it was suggested that, as he was in King's College War Studies Department, we had to put his talk into context with Clausewitz: there had to be a political dimension to any war and, by implication, the use of directed violence to support that. So, he was asked about the people in FATA; what was their political objective?

He did not seem immediately prepared to answer that question, but eventually he said, 'On reflection, I think they just want to be left alone.'

There is another aspect of security perhaps less studied but just as important, that is *objective security* – free *to* as opposed to free *from*. *Free to* would be for the polity to organise society as its members want; to agree the balance of public spending versus private enterprise for example and, internationally, to enter into agreements, pacts or treaties with other polities with respect to trade or, more particularly, security arrangements. *Objective security* also means the freedom to pursue a chosen way of life, to pursue the kind of life the populace wants; to learn, to save, to invest and generally to improve the population's lot.

CONCLUSIONS

There is only limited consensus as to the general causes of war. Identifying any common origins for an activity that has endured since the dawn of civilisation and has covered a world ruled by spears, bows, arrows and swords right through to supersonic planes, drones and nuclear weapons is bound to present an enormous challenge. It is also difficult to differentiate the root causes of wars and what *occasioned* any particular war. For example, there are many opinions as to the *causes* of the First World War but it is well known what occasioned it: the assassination of Archduke Franz Ferdinand and his wife, Countess Sophie, in Sarajevo in June 1914. Every war is unique in the sense that no two states or polities have an identical geopolitical situation, ideology, form of government or culture. No two states or polities will have the same perceptions of their security as their neighbour or possible enemy. No two states or polities will have the same interests and they will almost inevitably have different views about their honour, as illustrated by Germany in the First and Second World Wars (although in the latter case, grossly manipulated by Hitler) and by Japan in the Second World War. There is, simply, no one clear answer.

The decision to go to war, even defensively, is a dynamic invoked by a political leadership and advised, encouraged or discouraged by civil servants in some cases, political advisors in others and, sometimes, by the military. The decision may be informed by inaccurate or deliberately misleading intelligence. There is also the ever-present possibility of simple errors. From then on, any war might take on a life of its own, the original objective neglected, the political leadership unsure about how to progress but reluctant to admit it, even to themselves, and the military distracted by the sheer administrative burden of running a military operation.

The International system or world public opinion will also have a bearing. The US does not have the same view as China on the subject of maritime rights of passage in the China Seas; British Muslims did not have the same view of the UK's adventures in Iraq or Afghanistan, considering it, if not 'anti-Muslim', then at least demonstrating a stark lack of comprehension about those societies.

Perhaps the best that can be said is that, against a background of our four factors and within an International System, which may appear to be consistently followed but with dissenters, war is invoked within a framework of fear, interest and honour. Whereas we might be confident of our own case, of our own fears, interests and honour, there must be a good understanding of the other's point of view, something often forgotten. Let us not call the other the enemy just yet.

ADDENDUM TO CHAPTER 3: CAUSES OF WAR;
CAUSES OF PEACE
'ACCIDENTAL' OR 'SILLY' WARS
Some wars simply defy any logical analysis as to causes. They may be called 'Accidental' or 'Silly' Wars. Although some may be triggered by accidents or misunderstandings and some for absurd reasons, there is often an underlying cause, however obscure.

THE WAR OF JENKINS' EAR (1739)
Spanish privateers – legalised pirates, basically – boarded the Royal Navy brig, *Rebecca*, skippered by Robert Jenkins and cut off his left ear, accusing him of smuggling. The Spanish captain said – 'Go, and tell your King that I will do the same, if he dares to do the same.'

At the time no one was much bothered about Jenkins or his ear, but after Jenkins, in a nice piece of theatre, showed his decomposing ear to Parliament in 1738, opposition politicians and the British South Sea Company played up the insult to His Majesty and to Britain, hoping to foment war with Spain, both to win trade in the Caribbean and to guarantee British slave traders rights to sell slaves in Spanish America. They succeeded.

The war was subsumed in 1740 by the wider War of the Austrian Succession. It was prosecuted by Commodore George Anson who led his force across the Pacific. The war made Anson's name, however. He set off in 1740 to attack Spanish possessions in Central America, captured a million gold coins from an enemy galleon, and returned home nearly four years later having circumnavigated the globe. The fact that he lost nine tenths of his men from disease was forgotten. He was rich and was made First Lord of the Admiralty.

'ACCIDENTAL' OR 'SILLY' WARS: SPANISH–AMERICAN
WAR (1898)

The Spanish–American war originated in the Cuban struggle for independence from Spain, which began in February 1895. Spain's repressive measures were colourfully exaggerated by the American yellow press (newspapers that presented ill-researched news or sensationalist articles – particularly the Randolph Hearst papers), breeding anti-Spanish fervour. The spark was an explosion that sank the American battleship *USS Maine* in Havana harbour. She had been sent to protect US citizens and property after anti-Spanish rioting in Havana. Though the likely culprit was not a Spanish mine nor sabotage but an internal explosion, the US press proclaimed *Remember the Maine!* and the momentum for war was unstoppable. The war was wholly one-sided; Spain was incapable of fighting a major power so far away. A defeated Spain renounced all claim to Cuba, ceded Guam and Puerto Rico to the United States and transferred sovereignty over the Philippines to the USA for $20 million (worth $610 million today) and all because of a big bang they hadn't even ignited.

'ACCIDENTAL' OR 'SILLY' WARS: WAR OF THE STRAY DOG (1925)
A Greek–Bulgarian crisis (yet another; they were famous for them) was started in 1925 by a dog. Tension between Greece and Bulgaria had been simmering since the start of the 20th century, with rivalry over the possession of Macedonia and later Western Thrace. A Greek captain had an unruly pet dog, which, ignorant of the meaning of borders, ran into Bulgaria, with the Greek soldier giving chase. A Bulgarian sentry shot him (the Greek not the dog). The shooting became a rallying cry for the Greeks, who briefly invaded Bulgaria and occupied several villages. The League of Nations eventually imposed a ceasefire, but not before fifty deaths, all because of an ill-trained dog.

'ACCIDENTAL' OR 'SILLY' WARS: THE FOOTBALL WAR (1969)
Fought between El Salvador and Honduras after rioting at both home and away legs of a FIFA 1970 World Cup qualifier, the underlying cause was bitterness felt by El Salvador, a much smaller country than Honduras but with a larger population, as some 300,000 of their nationals were being booted out of neighbouring Honduras where they'd gone to work on the land (they made up 20% of the population). Land not owned by the bullying US corporation, United Fruit, which had effectively dictated the policy, was given to native Hondurans. The war began on 14 July 1969 with a Salvadoran attack on Honduras. It lasted one hundred hours before a ceasefire was brokered by the Organization of American States. Oh ... and El Salvador won the decisive third game 3–2 after extra time.

'ACCIDENTAL' OR 'SILLY' WARS: SUEZ (1956)

'Suez' is mentioned several times during this book and its importance in modern British history is worthy of explanation.

The Suez Canal was opened in 1869 and provided a direct route between the Mediterranean and the Red Sea and thus the Indian Ocean. The canal represents a border between Africa and Asia. It was of considerable utility to both the British in getting to India and to the French, with whom it was jointly owned, in getting to Indochina, saving nearly 9,000 km on the trip round the Cape. Hitherto, the journey had entailed a steamer voyage to Alexandria, a mule (later, train) journey to Port Suez and then another steamer onward.

In 1956, Gamal Abdel Nasser, the Egyptian president, nationalised it, an event that led to the 'Suez Crisis'. At the direction of the Prime Minister, Sir Anthony Eden, and in conjunction with French and Israeli troops, British forces invaded Egypt, seeking to take back control of the canal, and, indeed, Egypt. (Britain had virtually run Egypt before the Second World War.) The American president, Eisenhower, was incensed. When the attack started, he rang Eden and said, 'Anthony, have you gone off your head?' Eden was not a well man, but this was no excuse; what were his Cabinet doing? Eisenhower threatened a run on the pound and harassed Royal Navy ships in the Mediterranean. Britain backed down and withdrew her troops. Egypt kept the canal.

A recently declassified report in the National Archives, *Suez Operations in the Eastern Mediterranean*, refers to *the impossibility of success without American support*. Eden not only ignored this, but kept the Americans in the dark about the whole operation.

They were not fooled, the CIA having alerted Eisenhower to the British, French and Israeli antics. Eden was forced to resign and was replaced by Harold Macmillan.

The Suez débacle was a watershed moment for Britain and there was a multitude of consequences. It further weakened American confidence in British diplomacy, which had suffered after the Burgess and Maclean spy affair in 1951. The US came to regard the UK intelligence services as riddled with spies.

Britain's impotence had been demonstrated by the 1953 CIA coup in Iran, where British influence was supposed to hold sway, overthrowing the democratically elected Prime Minister, Mohammad Mosaddegh. The US–Iran relationship is still one based on mutual suspicion, which is well known, and Iranians are still suspicious of the UK, which is less well known. While the world was distracted by Suez, the Soviet Union invaded Hungary to quash its revolution, resulting in 16,000 casualties, including 6,000 dead.

Suez marked the end of Imperial Britain. From then on, Britain's foreign policy was subservient to that of the US and, although Harold Wilson refused to send troops to Vietnam, it led inexorably to Britain supporting the US in Security Council resolutions and ultimately to British participation in the invasion of Iraq in 2003. It may also have contributed to Brexit. In a speech at West Point on 5 December 1962, Dean Acheson, one-time United States Secretary of State, suggested that Great Britain 'has lost an Empire and has not yet found a role.'

There is another twist: in 1968 (a few weeks after the devaluation of the pound – another British drubbing), the UK government announced that within three years British forces would be withdrawn from military bases in Southeast Asia, Malaysia and Singapore, as well as the Persian Gulf and the Maldives. The phrase *East of Suez* entered the vernacular. Though one might allow that foreign policy must be essentially contingent, since the chronic problem with the UK governments of whatever stripe has been budget, it is now curious to see military activity creeping back to *East of Suez*.

In 2013 RUSI published a report indicating that Britain was in the process of a strategic shift back to an *East of Suez* position. A permanent military presence was being established by the RAF at Al Minhad in the United Arab Emirates and there was a continuing build-up of British troops in the Persian Gulf states. This coincided with establishment of the Royal Navy's UK Maritime Component Command (UKMCC) in Bahrain.

In 2014, the Foreign and Commonwealth Office announced that the UK would expand its naval facilities in Bahrain to support larger Royal Navy ships deployed to the Persian Gulf. HMS Jufair is the UK's first permanent military base located east of Suez since it withdrew from the region in 1971.

RATIONALITY AND WAR: JAPAN'S DECISION FOR WAR IN 1941

On 7 December 1941, 353 Japanese seaborne fighters attacked the US Pacific Fleet Headquarters at Pearl Harbor, Oahu, Hawaii. It was a surprise attack on a neutral country at that time. Japan intended the attack as a preventive strike to keep the United States from taking military actions against them in Southeast Asia. Eight US Navy battleships were damaged, with four sunk. 2,403 Americans were killed and 1,178 others were wounded. Japan announced a declaration of war on the United States later that day. The following day, the US Congress declared war on Japan. President Franklin D Roosevelt proclaimed December 7th 1941 as 'a date which will live in infamy' because the attack was made without a declaration of war and without explicit warning.

Tactically, it was one of the most brilliantly planned and splendidly executed exercises of the entire Second World War. But not quite: Admiral Nagumo's failure to destroy the naval base and to find and sink the US carriers was Japan's greatest blunder of the Pacific war. Destruction of the base or invasion of Hawaii – perfectly feasible if the army hadn't been distracted by possible war against the Russians – would have added another 3,000 miles sailing for the US Navy and would have cut the lifeline to Australia. Yamamoto's objective at Pearl Harbor was too limited: a flanking attack to knock out the US Pacific Fleet for six months so that Japan could conquer Southeast Asia unhindered. Thus, it secured an expensive inconvenience for the US rather than the hoped-for knockout blow.

Strategically, therefore, the assault on Pearl Harbor was a

complete and utter disaster for Japan and condemned that country to nearly four years of suffering and over five million deaths. The war culminated in the devastation of the atomic bombs dropped on Hiroshima and Nagasaki in August 1945.

Americans at the time called the attack 'strategic imbecility' and the Japanese 'stark, raving mad'.

Was there any logic in this disastrous attack? Does anything about it fit with Thucydides' concept of fear, interest and honour? Certainly, there was Japan's cultural need for national glory (honour), respect and for crucial raw materials (interests) via the conquest of east and Southeast Asia. They feared economic destruction by the US. The problem for the Japanese was that they confused honour with interest. They were driven by a sense of themselves as a great nation with an ancient heritage and deserving of respect. There was fault on the American side too: they too were guilty of terrible miscalculation; they were as culturally ignorant of Japan as the Japanese were of them.

FDR thought that no sensible Japanese leader could contemplate war with the mighty USA. He ignored any possible Japanese retaliation for his imposition of a complete trade embargo in the summer of 1941, which deprived Japan of eighty per cent of its oil needs and confronted Tokyo with a hard choice: submit to US demands, give up empire and resume economic dependency on the US or advance into Southeast Asia, with its crucial resources, and be economically independent.

Roosevelt's pre-war diplomacy was naïve. He demanded that Japan get out of China and Indochina. They had invaded Manchuria in 1931 and French Indochina in 1940. It was as much about the 'loss of face' – honour – for the Japanese as the loss of access to natural resources.

There is no common standard for rationality. For Hitler it was rational to invade Russia, for Lebensraum (living space). We might disagree. Truman's decision to cross the 38th Parallel in Korea in 1950 and provoking China, Johnson's committing combat forces to Vietnam in 1965, Bush's invasion of Iraq in 2003 were all considered rational by those presidents.

Churchill's decision to fight on after Dunkirk seems supremely irrational. 'Irrational stubbornness,' Max Hastings has called it. But Churchill had reasoned that if Britain fought and lost, she would receive terms much the same as if she had meekly surrendered. Luckily Hitler's and Tojo's monumental blunders, bringing in America and Russia into the war, saved Churchill's bacon. The Confederacy's decision to fight on in 1865 was dictated purely by honour; by any rational criterion, it was already beaten.

Two final thoughts on one of the most interesting exploits of the war: Roosevelt called the Japanese attack on Pearl Harbor 'unprovoked'. Was it? By placing a lethal economic noose around Japan's neck to punish Tokyo for aggression, the United States sought to stop Japan without a war. They ended up provoking one.

On the other hand and on the other side of the world, Churchill was delighted. America had joined in the war. Now he couldn't lose. His gamble of 1940 had paid off.

4. THE INTERNATIONAL CONTEXT

Academics and think-tanks aside, most people, politicians included, imagine that the International System, the bodies, laws, treaties, unions, alliances and conventions that govern international relations, is a constant rather than the result of painstaking and often painful, political, diplomatic and legal work, much of which started after the carnage of the Second World War. The West finds it difficult to imagine what life, international and domestic, would be like without those foundations. Yet given China and other Asian countries' resurgence (Russia is only a small player, despite its enormous size), this Western model may not persist. War does not happen in isolation, and we need to recognise fully the international context and how it might change. Is the West ready? The International System is a whole array of arrangements, a complete account of which would consume a whole library. For our purposes, however, we can condense this down to just seven key aspects:

1. Westphalia and the state system
2. Anarchy
3. The current International System
4. The United Nations
5. NATO and The European Union
6. Security Treaties
7. NGOs (Non-Governmental Organisations)

WESTPHALIA AND THE STATE SYSTEM
The Thirty Years' War was an epic and tragic series of wars that consumed the whole of Europe between 1618 and 1648. The death toll was horrendous and encompassed military and civilian casualties;

violence and famine wiped out as much as fifty per cent of the European population. However, an attempt to establish some lasting order did emerge from the carnage. The war ended with a series of treaties known as the Westphalian Peace. This established the state system and the idea of the independence of individual states, free from interference from other states, particularly on the subject of religion. It is a system that is still current, although slightly compromised by the UN-inspired Responsibility to Protect and by transnational intra-governmental, non-governmental and commercial operations. For the study of war, the most usual form of polity is the nation state, which indicates a certain coherence, recognition and objectives within that polity. It assumes that the population of that nation state, polity or proto-state is capable of concerted action. For the sake of clarity, and mentioned in the previous section, the Confederacy in the southern United States and the FLN in Algeria would fit a description of proto-state, whereas the Palestinians, with multiple territories and poor leadership, might just miss it.

THE THIRTY YEARS' WAR (1618–1648)

Although nothing like the Mongol invasions of China and Asia, which killed tens of millions of people, The Thirty Years' War was one of history's most brutal wars and was fought mostly in central Europe. There were 8 million casualties, less from battles than from resulting famine and disease. Almost all European countries were involved, not always on the side they started with.

The war ended with the Westphalian Peace which was the basis for the modern nation state, still current today.

For a full account of the 30 years' war, see the addendum to this chapter.

ANARCHY

We cannot contemplate the several or many causes of what war is all about without recognising the anarchic nature of the International System and the relationships between states. Political scientists define anarchy in international relations as the absence of any authority superior to nation states and capable of arbitrating their disputes, and thereby enforcing international law. It also means the absence of the rule of law or of stable global government. There are 195 or 196 countries in the world (Taiwan's status as an independent country is disputed by China), of which 193 are United Nations members. Strictly speaking, these countries co-relate in a state of anarchy. However, there is a great wealth of international law and, as many trade negotiations demonstrate, *most* countries follow *most* of international law *most* of the time. Even when there is a likelihood of war, other parties such as the United Nations, the European Union, ASEAN or the African Union might intervene and attempt to negotiate between the parties.

The Nuremberg trials of Nazi leaders (1945 to 1946) established the principle of 'waging aggressive war', and more recently there have been successful prosecutions in the International Criminal Court in The Hague of what are now regarded as war criminals: political or military leaders who have knowingly (it is alleged ...) practised murder or genocide or killed or captured prisoners or civilians.

However, it is recognised by the UN Charter that countries have a right to self-defence. They may, under international law, resort to military force to resist an attacker. Its relevance to the causes of war question is in the interpretation of *self-defence*. A couple of examples will illustrate this. Israel has a right to defend itself against armed attack with lethal force, as several wars with its Arab neighbours have illustrated. Implicit in this is that attacker should be another polity, but whether they have a right of self-defence against the Palestinians and people they nominally control with lethal force is less clear. To take this example further, do the Palestinians, who may constitute a 'polity' yet do not represent an actual nation state, have a right to defend themselves against the Israeli Defence Force? Similarly, with the Kurds, who occupy an independent region in northern Iraq and, to a lesser extent, Turkey, Syria and Iran. Though nominally under the control of the Baghdad (Iraqi) government, they are quasi-independent. In the event of armed aggression against them, do they have the right of self-defence? Suppose the attack was by forces of the Baghdad government? And, here we have an even bigger question: does this present the right to a pre-emptive strike?

The 'right of conquest' was traditionally a principle of international practice, rather than law that gave rights to a conqueror over countries or territories taken by military means. This has now given way, after its proscription after the Second World War, to the Nuremberg Principles and then, via the non-binding United Nations General Assembly Resolution 3314.

THE CURRENT INTERNATIONAL SYSTEM

The current international order was established by the victorious Allies: the US, USSR, China and the UK (France's involvement was a consolation prize) after the Second World War. It embodied a complex of international organisations and regulations that attempted to resolve the problems that had caused the Second World War and has proven robust enough to guide the world to the present day. For our purposes, we need to consider the several main structures: the United Nations System, NATO and similar bodies and non-governmental bodies – NGOs. They interact through diplomacy, bilateral agreements and through the UN itself. We should also add efforts by the United States to control nuclear weapons through multiple treaties and NGOs. Although this is an international concern, the United States takes the lead and involves other countries and other bodies on an occasional basis.

THE UNITED NATIONS

The UN was set up in 1945 after the horrendous carnage of World War II. It was and remains dedicated to international peace and stability. It originally had just fifty-one member states. Today, the organisation has 193 members, reflecting the number of new states, mainly former colonies and dependencies, since then. Its mandate was and remains to take initiatives aimed at preventing conflict and to provide humanitarian support to refugees and where the supply of food is interrupted. The UN suffers almost constant criticism for its bureaucracy, alleged wastefulness and ineffectiveness but, by and large, it has been successful. It has occasionally not seen eye to eye with the United States, which tends to regard it as a wayward extension of the State Department, and

The signing of the UN Charter, San Francisco, 1945. The start of the great experiment, still in progress…

with other powerful members such as China and Russia, which are suspicious of UN interference. Many of the UN's weaknesses stem from the nature of the Security Council, its highest authority, where the five permanent members, the US, the UK, Russia, China and France, do not hesitate to exercise their veto to defend their own interests, even when the wider international community thinks differently. Most of all, the United Nations is a *system* and, although, for example the World Bank does not have the same governance arrangements as the United Nations, it is still part of the whole structure and system, as is to some extent the International Monetary Fund (IMF). The UN's great achievement over the years has been to survive.

The UN contributes to peace in many ways, through various organs and specialised agencies, which cover many aspects of international affairs. These include, among others: Development, Refugees, Environmental Protection, Food and Agriculture, World Health and Women's Rights. All these contribute to maintaining peace in their own way. Prosperous societies are less likely to engage in internecine war than poorer states, provided there is a reasonably equitable distribution of wealth in terms of wages and social goods. The UN's involvement in avoiding – or at the very least *managing* – war centres on dialogue. The General Council of the UN is a forum where every country is represented and any accusation and rebuttal must be made in public. The General Council may then pass a resolution (all are available on the UN website), but they generally carry less weight than do Security Council Resolutions. The SC has only fifteen members – the five permanent members (the victorious Allied powers of World War II) and ten others chosen by rota.

The second valuable contribution that the United Nations makes to peace is through Peacekeeping Operations. The UN Department Action for Peacekeeping (A4P) has the best description of its own work:

UN Peacekeeping helps countries navigate the difficult path from conflict to peace. We have unique strengths, including legitimacy, burden sharing, and an ability to deploy troops and police from around the world, integrating them with civilian peacekeepers to address a range of mandates set by the UN Security Council and General Assembly.

Peacekeeping may not be well understood. The basic premise is that *you can't keep the peace if there is no peace to keep.* Peacekeepers, who are troops from other countries, are guided by three principles: the consent of both sides in a conflict, impartiality and the non-use of force except in self-defence. They facilitate, for example, peace talks – particularly useful where, although both sides want peace, there is not enough confidence to believe that they can meet in peace and agree any sort of concord. Having impartial peacekeepers *in the room* facilitates this.

The UN model represents the concept of liberal Western values and its attributes such as freedom, democracy, capitalism and free trade and works to a rules-based System. A prospective problem is that we in the West imagine that this model is the only system going. It is becoming increasingly obvious that other countries do not share this view, the most notable examples being Russia and China, which causes the West some confusion and suspicion. Challenges are also coming from newly emerging states, from electorates who might feel disenfranchised and from the growth of social media, spreading dubiously sourced 'news' or highly opinionated gossip. Overall, though, the whole system has had a greatly positive impact on global security and prosperity. The great triumph of the United Nations is to have survived for seventy-five years. It is still respected, despite some nay-sayers, and can be relied upon as a forum for the discussion of potential conflict and for the provision of peacekeepers and humanitarian aid. Should the UN collapse, it would be greatly missed.

NATO

The North Atlantic Treaty Organization, is an intergovernmental political-military alliance created in 1949 by the USA, Great Britain, Canada and nine other European countries. NATO created a system of collective defence where each of the sovereign member states agreed to come to the aid of each other in the event of an attack by any external party. To all intents and purposes, this meant the Soviet Union. NATO now comprises twenty-nine countries, with another four as aspiring members. Over the years, NATO has had a tortuous journey through a long succession of directional and policymaking initiatives including the Petersberg Tasks, the Helsinki Headline Goal, the Berlin Plus Agreement, and dozens and dozens of high-level meetings, some nugatory. NATO members are obliged – sort of – to spend two per cent of GDP on defence. Currently, only the US, the UK (given a bit of creative accounting) and Greece achieve this.

NATO SAYS IT HAS TWO ROLES:

A political role: *NATO promotes democratic values and encourages consultation and cooperation on defence and security issues to build trust and, in the long run, prevent conflict.*

A military role: *NATO is committed to the peaceful resolution of disputes. If diplomatic efforts fail, it has the military capacity needed to undertake crisis-management operations.*

So far, so good, one might think, but it is not a view shared by many academics and think-tankers. Over the years, there have been many adverse comments and articles of which a typical example might be Professor Andrew Dorman's article in *International Affairs*, March 2012: *NATO's 2012 Chicago summit: a chance to ignore the issues once again?*

NATO was set up largely to counter the Soviet Union and what was thought of as their hegemonic ambitions. The first Secretary General, the British general Lord 'Pug' Ismay, who had been Winston Churchill's chief military assistant during the Second World War, said before he took his post that NATO was created to 'keep the Soviet Union out, the Americans in, and the Germans down.'

Set up in 1949 as a military / political alliance of American and European allies. Badly mauled in Afghanistan (2000 to 2020), and called 'brain dead' by French President Macron, its function and future are constantly debated, but then that was always the case. With no alternative European concept, NATO will endure, even if it simply allows Europeans to talk to the Americans

And so it remains, although, despite occasional flurries of concern about the Baltic states, the Russians no longer need 'keeping out' and the Germans no longer need 'keeping down'. However, given the lack of consensus and coordination within European countries, there is still a desperate need to keep the Americans 'in'. In fact, it's not too much of a stretch to say that being able to talk to the Americans through NATO is one of its most important benefits to Europeans. Russia continues to oppose further NATO expansion, seeing it as inconsistent with informal understandings between Soviet leader Mikhail Gorbachev and European and US negotiators that allowed for a peaceful German reunification in 1990.

THE EUROPEAN UNION
The European Union (EU) is a political and economic union of twenty-seven member states in Europe, grown out of the Treaty of Rome of

Starting as the European Coal and Steel Community, it developed into the EEC (European Economic Community), and then eventually the European Union. Although a member for many years, the United Kingdom was always semi-detached, with a misconceived idea that they were superior to Europeans (actually, to foreigners in general). In a referendum in 2016, United Kingdom voted to leave the European Union (Brexit) to great lamentations from many informed and honest commentators

1957, and set up originally as six countries, led by France and Germany. The essential idea was to prevent war between the two (France and Germany had gone to war in 1870, 1914 and 1940) but its expression came to be and remains largely about trade and the free movement of people, goods and capital. The EU also has foreign policy, security and defence aspirations. The Common Security and Defence Policy (CSDP) is part of the EU's Common Foreign and Security Policy (CFSP). So in many respects this reflects similar aspirations to those of the UN and NATO. The UN itself can, in theory at least, call on all 196 members, NATO on all 29 members, and the EU on all 27. There is, of course, much overlap, although the EU military structures are smaller than those of NATO.

On 8 July 2016, the President of the European Council and the President of the European Commission, together with the Secretary General of the NATO signed a Joint Declaration in Warsaw with a view to giving new impetus and new substance to the EU–NATO strategic partnership. Notwithstanding, the EU and NATO don't get on. Now if this were a matter of some minor trade policy issue or some product specification, one might be able to accept some confusion and delay. But here, we are talking about Europe's and the UK's security, particularly in the light of a resurgent Russia, and various other trouble spots in Europe's 'near abroad', such as Lebanon, Israel / Palestine, the Sahel and, a long-dormant problem, Spanish Sahara / Morocco.

In terms of funding, former US President Trump not unreasonably wanted more of a contribution from the other members of NATO. The US spends about 3% of its GDP on defence, the rest of NATO regularly less than the 2% agreed and the EU, on average, about the same or less. There may also be a suspicion that Trump, who saw international relations as a zero-sum game, viewed Europe, manifest in the European Union, as a competitor. One result of this is that other NATO members have grown less confident in America's commitment to European defence, particularly in the light of Turkey's (a NATO member) wayward foreign policy.

It is extraordinarily difficult to shine a light down these dark corridors. One well-respected and well-resourced think-tank, the Brookings Institution in Washington DC, talks of 'the lack of communication between NATO and the European Union even though these vital Western institutions are located just a few miles from each other' (in Brussels).

Lack of communication! More damningly, Brookings assert that 'there is a striking absence of policy coordination between them'. Well, there wouldn't be, would there, if they don't talk? This is despite the observations about the CSDP and CFSP above. And from an examination of the Joint Declaration in July 2016, we can pick out the rather floppy verbs that head each section: Boost, Broaden, Expand, Develop, Facilitate, Step up, Build, which wouldn't pass muster in an undergraduate international relations class. Brookings goes on to point out that twenty-two of the other twenty-eight (excluding the US) NATO countries also belong to the EU. There is a general and well-founded concern that if the US retreats into 'not quite' isolationism, it will leave something of a leadership vacuum. Better relations would benefit both parties and particularly a Brexited UK.

NGOS (NON-GOVERNMENTAL ORGANISATIONS)

The term *NGO* covers a vast array of organisations of all sizes, both domestic and international, and all involved in one way or another in improving the lives of those less fortunate. They generally work in humanitarian and social areas and have been increasingly active since the end of the Second World War. As the name implies, they are independent of government, though there is often an element of government funding. Many are also funded by private donations and various charitable trusts. Their key attribute is that they are not only independent of government but maintain absolute neutrality in the face of conflict. The ICRC, more popularly known as the Red Cross (or the Red Crescent in Islamic countries), is absolute in its neutrality and it was one of the few bodies that were able to deliver parcels to prisoners of war during the world wars of the 20th century. Surveys suggest that NGOs enjoy a high degree of public trust, which make them a useful, if not always sufficient, proxy for the concerns of society and stakeholders. Our interest here is in those NGOs that work to prevent war, those offering conciliation to both sides during conflict or those working in the post-conflict period, establishing such as a constitutional settlement or electoral reform. Such is the vast span of NGO work that a few examples will illustrate their work in the area of war and peace. For UK NGOs only and from their own websites:

International Alert was founded in 1986 to help people find peaceful solutions to conflict. Although the number of conflicts between countries was decreasing, there was an alarming increase in the number of conflicts *within* countries. This led to gross violations of human rights. IA work in this area in training and facilitation.

OXFAM is about alleviating poverty, worldwide. It works in the areas of food, water, health and education, women's rights, businesses and property, aid and development, citizens' rights and climate change. They are best known for saving lives and providing aid in a crisis, such as conflicts and natural disasters.

NGOs do not provide any constraint on war *per se*. They do not have recourse to armed force, although they may request Peace Support operational troops to deliver humanitarian aid. NGOs will always be available as arbitrators before and during a conflict, for the provision of aid during a conflict and for help in peace-building after a conflict. They work largely through providing a basis for peace in the form of education, microfinance, improvements to civil society, a more equitable constitution, a free press (with its concomitant competent journalists) and so on.

PEACE AND SECURITY TREATIES

The 20th century also saw three other less successful attempts to provide security and to limit and control war. After the First World War, the American president Woodrow Wilson attended the Paris Peace Conference of 1919 and 1920, aka the Versailles Peace Conference. Rather too early in the proceedings, he proposed his now famous, or possibly infamous, Fourteen Points. Eight of these pertained to specific countries – Russia, Belgium and others; some pertained to general international issues, such as free trade: two are of particular interest.

The first, Point 5, specified that: *Colonized people must have an equal voice as the governing country.* This has been used by many breakaway or secessionist polities to justify rebellion or insurrection.

Once regarded as one of America's most cherished and progressive presidents, Wilson is now increasingly thought of as something of a pariah (the first southern president since the Civil War had views on race that would be regarded as unconscionable today and he famously enthused over DW Griffith's film, *Birth of a Nation*, which glorified the Ku Klux Klan). But he did propose Point 14: *A general association of nations must be formed under specific covenants for the purpose of affording mutual guarantees of political independence and territorial integrity to great and small states alike.* This was the provenance of the League of Nations, a forerunner to the United Nations. Tragically, the USA never joined. At the outset of the Second World War, it was generally thought that the League had failed to prevent World War II – although nothing was going to stop Hitler. With that, and the absence of the US, the League effectively fell apart in 1939. However, the League's legacy was the United Nations.

THE LOCARNO TREATIES

Versailles was reinforced by the Locarno Treaties, negotiated in Switzerland in October 1925. At the time, people talked positively and warmly of the 'Spirit of Locarno'. The treaties stated that the Western European Allied powers and the Central and Eastern European states wished to secure a post-war territorial settlement and return to normal relations with the successor of the defeated German Reich, the Weimar Republic. Tellingly, the eastern borders of Germany with Poland were left open for revision.

THE KELLOGG-BRIAND PACT

Another example of an attempt to moderate war through a Peace or Security Treaty was the Kellogg-Briand Pact, an international agreement negotiated between US Secretary of State, Frank Kellogg, and French Foreign Minister, Aristide Briand, in 1928. Signatory states promised not to use war to resolve their differences. It was signed by Germany and France (at war twelve years later), and the United States (Germany declared war on the US in 1941, just after Pearl Harbor). There were no mechanisms for enforcement. Similar concepts were incorporated into the UN Charter and the pact remains in effect today.

Overall, treaties can cover almost any aspect of the relationship between two or more states: trade, defence, borders, migration, citizenship – the list goes on. But security treaties do not generally contribute to security or to inhibiting a war. Neither Versailles nor the League of Nations prevented the Second World War. The German–Soviet non-aggression pact, the Molotov–Ribbentrop Pact of August 1939, was broken less than two years later when Nazi Germany invaded Soviet Russia in 1941. Even then, not all security treaties are the same and there is no general model. Treaties may be negotiated as a solution to a problem or with a greater or lesser degree of coercion. Such pacts have largely gone out of fashion since the end of the Second World War. They never did have much success anyway.

LEGAL FRAMEWORKS FOR WAR

Aside actual international pacts, there have been attempts over the years to regularise war or provide some protection for civilians, injured combatants and prisoners of war. There's a bit in the Bible, but not much of interest. In mediaeval times, the Roman Catholic Church thought about 'just war', but it was Hugo Grotius who wrote two books of note: *The Free Seas* (1609) and *On the Law of War and Peace* (1625). There was passing interest in the nineteenth century but it was not until the twentieth century that any laws of war had any real traction. It's easy to confuse the various laws, conventions and 'custom and practice', but the following are of note:

The **Hague Conventions of 1899 and 1907** rest on five fundamental principles that are inherent: military necessity, unnecessary suffering, proportionality, discrimination, and honour (chivalry).

The **Geneva Conventions of 1906 and 1929** produced, in particular, the *Humanitarian Law of Armed Conflicts*, concerning wounded or captured military personnel, medical personnel and non-military civilians during war or armed conflicts. While The Hague Conventions set out the rules for conducting war, the Geneva Conventions are designed to protect the *victims* of war.

The **European Convention on Human Rights (ECHR)** is the international convention intended to protect Human Rights and political freedoms and came into force in 1953.

The **Responsibility to Protect (RTP)** is intended to protect civilians in armed conflict and to protect populations from genocide, war crimes, ethnic cleansing and crimes against humanity. It was endorsed by the World Summit in 2005. It is a major contribution to international affairs, but not wholly effective.

CONSTRAINTS ON WAR

Even with its shortcomings and failures, we can now see the vital importance of the current International System and thereby the dangers of it becoming compromised. Domestic and international politics interact and influence each other, and we can identify six areas where politics and the social environment influence war (as a political act) compared, say, with the nineteenth century:

The end of territory as an expression of greatness. Imperialist wars were about expanding territory, influence and access to natural resources and markets. Hitler's attempted conquest of Russia was to gain *Lebensraum* (living space) for the German peoples as well as reflecting his hatred of Bolshevism, Jews and Slavs. Although some borders are still disputed, generally speaking, they are settling down. In Africa, one of the largest continents in the world, the Organisation of African States, predecessor to the African Union, agreed in 1964 that the borders between the fifty countries in Africa should stay with the old colonial model. The alternative was never-ending conflict about tribal areas, natural resources and access to the oceans.

Assumption against war and the invention of peace. It is tempting to start from the assumption that peace is the norm and war something of an aberration. Not quite. Sir Henry Maine was a 19th century comparative jurist and Regius Professor of Civil Law at Oxford. He observed that *war appears to be as old as mankind, but peace is a modern invention.* Certainly, some authorities claim that of the past 3,400 years, humans have been entirely at peace for 268 of them, or just eight per cent of recorded history.

War, like scandal, now happens in public. Media attention focuses on the pity of war, which is streamed into people's living rooms every evening. One of the reasons for America's failure in Vietnam was that the main news item every evening clearly demonstrated that they were losing the war. The flip side of this is, of course, compassion fatigue. One moment the media is focused on the tragedy of Syria, the next on the tragedy in Yemen. Little attention is given, or indeed has been given, to the similar wars in the Democratic Republic of Congo or the Central African Republic.

Cosmopolitanism. With the advent of easier and cheaper air travel, the notion of gap years for school leavers and international education schemes, the world has become more cosmopolitan. So instead of thinking of Hitler's schemes for Czechoslovakia as a 'quarrel in a faraway country, between people of whom we know nothing' (Neville Chamberlain in 1938), it would now be the home of, in the author's case, his mate, Roman.

Democracy is a big factor in war, though in most Western countries the democratic scrutiny of any decision to go to war is wholly inadequate. In other countries, there is no scrutiny at all. Examining some of the famous wars of the 20th century, there was actually very little consultation with the electorate about those war decisions. For example, in the United Kingdom, the decision to join the Americans in the invasion of Iraq was put to Parliament, who passed it with a clear majority, with most Labour MPs following the party line. Some authorities now suggest that every decision to deploy troops in any foreign action should only be permitted only after an un-whipped vote in Parliament.

There is now greater focus on war crimes. The International Criminal Court, which began functioning on 1 July 2002, now prosecutes alleged war criminals accused of wilful killing, torture and a lengthy list of other crimes. It has not been universally successful, but it represents a good start: military thugs can no longer be confident that they can get away with their horrendous acts. Unfortunately, not all countries recognise the ICC or are signatories to the convention.

Thus the causes of war, or certainly the excuses *for* war, are slowly being narrowed; aggressive leaders are being prosecuted and third parties, such as other countries or supra-national bodies are taking more of an interest. And, although there is much talk of the United Nations' impotence in dealing with continuing or incipient wars, war gets much more diplomatic attention.

In conclusion, given that the world has not seen any great power wars since 1945, that global trade has increased manyfold, that, despite many of the world's people still living in abject poverty, many people around the world now have better lives than hitherto and, most of all, that there is a general awareness of poverty, injustice and conflict, it is difficult to conclude anything but that the current International System has been a relative success.

Yet the West finds it difficult or even impossible to contribute to the conflicts in Syria or Yemen. Neither does the West have an answer to navigation rights in the South China Sea or the status of Taiwan. Even so, and even if the United States retreats into part isolation, there are many who think that this 'Western' International System is worth fighting for. Certainly, some parts of it are, but it may be that a new international system will emerge with different values than those reflected in our six constraints above. We can only be sure that one will survive: that of anarchy. But let us hope that others do too.

The transition will be difficult and may result in wars, possibly between major powers, with the nuclear danger ever present. In short, considering the question that was posed at the beginning of this chapter, the West is woefully unprepared for both frictional wars and for whatever new international system emerges.

ADDENDUM TO CHAPTER FOUR: THE INTERNATIONAL
CONTEXT
THE THIRTY YEARS' WAR (1618–1648)
This was one of history's most brutal wars and was fought mostly in central Europe. There were 8 million casualties, less from battles as from resulting famine and disease. It started as a war between Catholic and Protestant states of the Holy Roman Empire. However, as it evolved, it became less about religion and more about power and which group would dominate and govern Europe. It changed the geopolitical face of Europe and the role of both religion and nation states in society.

Bohemia, Sweden, Denmark, Norway, Spain, Austria and France were all involved, with various leagues and alliances in attendance. Of course, the Holy Roman Empire was a key player, but never forget Voltaire's verdict in 1756 that: 'The Holy Roman Empire was neither Holy nor Roman, nor an Empire.'

The reason it is important to us now is how it ended. In 1648, a series of treaties called the Peace of Westphalia effectively ended the Thirty Years' War, with significant geopolitical effects.

Spain lost its grip over Portugal and the Dutch Republic, but former Holy Roman Empire states won increased autonomy in German-speaking central Europe.

The legacy of the Thirty Years' War and the Westphalian Peace is that it laid the basis for the formation of the modern nation state, establishing fixed boundaries for the belligerent countries and decreeing that residents of a state were subject to the laws of that state, not to those of any other institution, secular or religious.

This radically altered the balance of power in Europe and severely restricted the influence of the Catholic Church, hitherto the dominant institution over political affairs.

5. POLITICS AND 'POLITICS'

Few people nowadays – politicians especially – give much thought to politics. This might seem an extraordinary assertion given the enormous coverage of the subject and the media's obsession with interviewing ignorant (in its literal sense of not knowing much) MPs about subjects they know even less about. Most – one is tempted to say *all* – politics is actually politicking, a contest between rival political parties for our vote. Real politics, on the other hand, is about how the citizens (although, of course, in the United Kingdom today, having left the European Union, we revert to being subjects) choose their form of government, determine how their leaders exercise power, decide 'who gets what' and how the wealth generated by the country gets distributed. In the United Kingdom today, we still have a similar form of government to the one we had hundreds of years ago. Despite promises to the contrary, the House of Lords remains substantially unreformed, though their power is considerably reduced. The House of Lords comprises a substantial proportion of landowners, religious leaders, judges, clerics, political appointees and even the son of an ex-KGB agent, all claiming their £305 a day (tax-free) and travelling expenses on top. In terms of power, it is now even more centralised on the prime minister, although when that post was instituted, it was a term of disdain. In terms of 'who gets what', the wealthy land-owning gentry are still with us, and bankers and hedge funds still make vast fortunes after playing around with citizens' (sorry, subjects') money – and when they lose it all, they simply take more. And, to coin a phrase, the poor are always with us. Now called 'essential workers', the working classes are now rebranded as 'hard-working families', which would be a masterly bit of marketing were it not so transparent.

BUT WHAT IS POLITICS?

Politics is a noble endeavour that operates in four domains: one theoretical and three practical. In the theoretical domain, politics is largely about philosophy, esoteric stuff which, despite some avowed allegiances, most politicians ignore. At one extreme, one could cite Karl Marx and other socialist writers like Antonio Gramsci, an Italian Marxist philosopher, or William Morris, who, as well as being a British textile designer, was a poet and socialist activist. In the other corner we have thinkers who see a 'laissez faire' or 'free market' approach as the answer to all problems: social, educational, industrial. Friedrich Hayek, an Austrian/British economist and philosopher, and Milton Friedman, an American economist, would fall into this camp. Neither extreme is ever realised. The old Soviet Union was nominally a socialist state but it failed to achieve Stalin's paradise, and much of the putative benefits of socialism went to the nomenklatura, who guarded their privileges closely. On the other side, if ever markets were 'free' and its concomitant concept 'capitalism' let rip, society would collapse.

In the first practical domain, politics is about how society orders itself; who shares in the benefits of being an organised society; who has access to power. It is also about governance, the process of exercising control through checks and balances on leaders and decision makers. It is based on a canon of law which, in most of the Western world at least, is democratically developed by an elected legislature and exercised by an independent judiciary. People challenged to define politics might only allude to the various political parties, reflected by their various extravagant claims, and the commentaries of political correspondents in the media. Much of this, though, is essentially *politicking* – the second, practical domain. The schoolboy heckling one hears during Prime Minister's Questions – and to a large extent in the press – is not designed to further political thinking as such, but to show the Prime Minister or

The United Kingdom of Great Britain and Northern Ireland's Houses of Parliament: 'The Mother of Parliaments'

the Leader of the Opposition in a better (or, in the case of Boris Johnson, worse) light for the benefit, in the first place, of the backbenchers, and in the second place the electorate. Mr Speaker receives thousands of letters every year complaining about unruly behaviour in the House, so it clearly does not impress the electorate. Politics and the media are especially disposed to label someone as right-wing, left-wing or centrist although, in the modern mixed economy based on state control and private enterprise, this definition is becoming increasingly blurred, irrelevant even. What, for instance, is a liberal? The English parliamentary system is essentially adversarial, as is our common law legal system. The role of the court in English law is to be an impartial referee between prosecution and defence. The English common law and parliamentary systems are distinct from various European countries with civil law systems, which are essentially inquisitorial. This means that European politics tends to be more consensual, and more likely to reach agreement through consensus, often with coalition government.

In the third, international domain, politics is about the inter-relationship between states: *International Relations.* International politics interacts with domestic politics in a complex, dynamic way: *foreign policy.* Insofar as the United Kingdom has a comprehensive foreign policy at all, this is not a subject which is generally debated by the electorate or even very much by Parliament. To be fair, there is significant work carried out by parliamentary committees, but a combination of the lack of time set aside to debate their recommendations in the House, the government's domination of foreign policy under its royal prerogative powers, and its tight control over parliamentary business, allows little effective parliamentary scrutiny. Thus, one might search in vain for any statement of the current government's foreign policy or for its policy on any particular issue. 'Perpetual interests' might surface from time to time, but that's about it. It is rare that UK foreign policy has gone against that of the United States. As a member of the United Nations Security Council, this is a something of an omission.

States co-exist in a condition of anarchy, where there is no higher power, so they do not face the same absolute restrictions as political leaders within states. There is, to be sure, a canon of international law, but obeying this is more to do with choice and peer pressure – that is, the views of other states – than obligation. In fact, most international law is followed. There are also of course various supra-national bodies, like the European Union and the United Nations and, whereas they do not have any absolute power as would, say, the police and courts in a particular state, they can yield considerable influence.

WAR IS POLITICS BY OTHER MEANS

This is a popular aphorism likely to raise something of a gallows laugh in a society largely uninterested in war or, for that matter, politics. It might invoke disgust among people who call themselves pacifists and to some it might provide evidence of militaristic cynicism. Its author was one Carl von Clausewitz, a Prussian military staff officer who had fought during the Napoleonic Wars. But it's not quite the original quote: the best interpretation (translated from the original High German) seems to be:

War is simply a continuation of political intercourse, with the addition of other means. War in itself does not suspend political intercourse or change it into something entirely different. It is essential that intercourse continues, irrespective of the means it employs.

Clausewitz devoted the latter part of his life, as Director of the Prussian War College, to ordering his thinking about war to provide some guide to thinking or a handbook for future generals and politicians. His magnum opus, *On War*, is a classic on the subject – one of few – and has been rediscovered only comparatively recently. To realise the full meaning of the statement *War is simply a continuation* ... and incidentally the richness of the whole of his treatise *On War*, we have to define the meaning of state, war and politics and understand what relevance this all has to the modern environment. Clausewitz's statement is of considerable profundity. What Clausewitz realised was that there has to be a *political settlement* in prospect to inform and direct any war. This is required even if it were a war of annihilation when, rather obviously, there would be no state left on the other side to worry about. He was also, by implication, writing about internal politics.

Although he lived in what would now be called a one-party state, he recognised that the will of the people was essential to wage war and

*The US Capitol Building, known as 'The Hill' just down the road from the White House,
contains both the House of Representatives and the Senate*

talked of their *primordial violence, hatred and enmity* for the enemy as
one factor in war, although this may have represented his feelings about
the French as much as anything else. Notwithstanding the political
circumstances *within* a state (Clausewitz was not concerned with
Prussia's political system), he recognised that if people were not prepared
to go to war in defence of their country, then they could not in the long
run be protected. On the other hand, if they were not prepared to accept
an alien conquest, then that occupation could not be sustained. War is
as much to do with defining society as it is to do with defining war itself.

Thus war, society and internal, practical politics, as much as
international relations, are inseparable and all interact with each other.
Because of this interrelationship, a fundamental tenet of the Western
democratic world is that the military should be directed by and answerable
to politicians, who represent society. It is politicians who wage war, not
servicemen and women. The military might prosecute war but the first

and last responsibility must remain with politicians. To Clausewitz this was an absolute given, although he qualified the relationship between military and politicians – in his case, a ruling monarch – in some depth. Military power is the most closely guarded prerogative of the ruling elite, be that the monarchy, an elected or imposed government or 'the Party'. Without society's backing, military force amounts simply to hired thugs – the Condottieri of the Italian Renaissance. There are other, less apparent dynamics to this relationship between politics, society and the military. The first is honour: servicemen and women are accorded high status within most societies and are put on their honour not to abuse their power. They swear allegiance to the state or ruling monarch. There is also an unstated fear that the military might usurp the state, as happened in Greece in 1967 when 'the Colonels' staged a coup d'état, and nearly in France in 1968 – only narrowly averted by Charles de Gaulle. Egypt 2013 is an example, as are numerous African countries since decolonisation. This is perhaps not something to which people in the UK or the US can easily relate; both countries have a military who are very unlikely to stage a coup.

War must have a political dimension. If there is no political dimension, it is not war; it is just violence and, under almost all systems of domestic, international and even religious law, illegal. Of course, legitimate, state-controlled military action is not only used against other states. The military has been preoccupied lately with 'counter-insurgency', where 'insurgents' – armed groups – challenge whatever legitimate government there is. These insurgents have a political agenda, as do terrorists, however distasteful it might be. Military power is also used against criminal organisations who may be acting like insurgents but, in the main, do not have a legitimate political agenda. To not have a political dimension would be instances where there was no political settlement in prospect, in the first instance *between* the combatant states but also *within* them. Let us look at one example where we can see the interplay of politics, society and the use of military force.

In April 1982, Argentina, then led by a military junta, invaded and captured the British territory of the Falkland Islands in the South Atlantic. The British Prime Minister, Margaret Thatcher, in conjunction with a newly formed War Cabinet, determined to recapture the islands. Public opinion did not, perhaps, reach the level of 'primordial violence, hatred and enmity', but there was genuine outrage in the UK against this illegal and unheralded act. On 1 May 1982, an RAF Vulcan bomber flew from Ascension Island, just off the coast of Africa, on an 8,000-nautical-mile round trip to the Falklands. The mission required repeated refuelling, including tanker-to-tanker refuelling, and was a triumph of RAF logistical planning. The Vulcan dropped a stick of bombs across the runway at Stanley. The Argentinians claimed that only one bomb struck the runway itself, and that this was quickly repaired. *Militarily* this had little effect on the occupation and it could be claimed that it was a considerable waste of valuable resources. However, *politically* it sent three important messages to the Argentinians. First, it emphasised that the United Kingdom was absolutely serious about re-taking the islands. In the words of the official historian of the Falklands War, Professor Sir Lawrence Freedman, once Margaret Thatcher had made up her mind, 'she did not look back'. Second, it confirmed that the RAF, based on Ascension, over 6,000 km away, could reach and hit the Falklands. It might be guessed that the Argentinians had an idea of the logistical challenges here, but nevertheless, they could not thereafter station their fast jets at Port Stanley airfield. This meant that, given the flying time from mainland Argentina to the Falklands, their fighters could only spend about ten to fifteen minutes over the islands. Third, it suggested that if the RAF could hit the Falklands, then they could hit mainland Argentina. In fact, the effect of this action was diminished when the

UK made clear that there would be no strikes on air bases in Argentina. Overall, the Falklands War illustrates the political and military interplay between the combatant states, the international relations aspect and the internal politics within both countries. Argentina had been in the midst of a devastating economic crisis and large-scale civil unrest against the junta and cynics say that Prime Minister Margaret Thatcher's motivation was a reflection of her low poll ratings at the time, but she had the country behind her.

War has three political dimensions: the relationship between states (international relations), the relationships between states and other political actors (intergovernmental bodies, such as the UN, the EU and NATO), and the state and its own body politic.

Wars can be started by a disaffected section of society but they are difficult to sustain: one factor in the UK recovery of the Falklands was domestic dissent in Argentina and some have attributed the collapse of the Soviet system in Russia to their debacle in Afghanistan between 1979 and 1989. Early in the Vietnam fiasco, diplomats judged that the political system of South Vietnam was inadequate to sustain a modern state – they could not even manage the US-designed communications system when the Americans left. Yet the war dragged on for years, and was only ended by US public opinion. Afghanistan was even worse: notwithstanding previous failed engagements by both Britain and Russia, it was well understood – or certainly should have been – that, like South Vietnam, the Afghan state, as a reflection of their society, was inadequate to the task of running a modern country, or anything else for that matter.

War is about more than the use of legitimate, controlled violence, and more than just 'winning' or 'losing'. War has its roots deep in society and whatever political system pertains. A war, however resolved, must satisfy the victors and at the very least placate the vanquished. Even then, no settlement is ever final. Greece was occupied by the Ottoman Turks for 300 years, and fought successfully for independence between 1821 and 1832. The Allies assumed that Germany had been 'beaten' in the First World War, although many if not all Germans themselves thought that they had just reached an armistice, a sort of 'score draw', which was ludicrous. Nevertheless, the Paris Peace Conference in 1919 imposed what the Germans thought were harsh conditions, allowing Hitler and the Nazi Party a route to power. In each case the determinants were international politics, domestic politics and the attitudes of the respective societies. *War is politics by other means* ... or rather *War is simply a continuation of political intercourse, with the addition of other means* ... can be seen as an expression of great profundity, a statement of the obvious or Jesuitical circular logic. Touching as it does on every aspect of civilisation, society and politics, it goes to the very heart of human existence: politics, truly defined.

6. STRATEGY AS THE LINK BETWEEN POLITICS AND THE USE OF ARMED FORCE

WHAT IS STRATEGY?

The word *strategy* is everywhere. Football coaches use it – wrongly – to describe how they're going to win the next game. David Attenborough uses it – correctly – to describe how some rodent lives in the middle of the African desert. And commercial enterprises use it to describe, sometimes correctly, sometimes with a little hyperbole, their future plans. Given that the first attempts at formalising strategic planning in business were based on the experience of Allied planning staffs during World War II, this wider use is understandable. But it is not conducted very effectively in the national or military sense. Strategy is a term used too widely, usually as an adjective (as in *strategic location*, whatever that may be) and often with the aspiration that the reader will imagine that some higher-level thinking has taken place. In essence, strategy is about reconciling ends, ways and means: the overall objectives; how we're going about achieving them; what resources we are going to commit.

In the example in the previous chapter concerning the Falklands War, the overall national *policy* was to maintain the integrity of the UK's overseas territories. Thus, the strategy, the *ends*, was to retake the Falklands; the *ways* were military; the *means* was the Royal Navy, supported by the British Army. The *strategy* could have been different: *ends* might have been to stabilise the occupation of the islands by Argentina while avoiding embarrassment to the UK government; the *ways* might have been an international treaty; the *means* might have been intense diplomatic activity, both inter-state and at the UN. There might also have been a Royal Naval blockade of Argentinian ports as a *way* of achieving that end.

In decisions about invoking and prosecuting war, the political and military should be closely integrated. This is not always the case. Depictions from the UK are rare. This is an example from Moldova; President Igor Dodon (centre) with military and ministers

Before moving on to the more practical aspects, it is worth looking at some strategic theory. We define theory as *a clear set of tested propositions, regarded as correct, that can provide explanation and prediction.* With scientific phenomena, a theory can be precisely defined and possibly proven. With social behaviour, a theory can only provide guidelines. There are many books and articles on the subject of strategy. Some get nowhere near any definition, some ramble on for page after page of what amounts to reflective thought. The late Colin Gray, one-time Professor of International Relations and Strategic Studies at the University of Reading, wrote many books and articles on the theory of strategy, outlining twenty-three *dicta* – useful for classroom discussions but rather unwieldy when a strategy is actually needed. He writes elsewhere of forty *maxims*, similar to dicta, which might be somewhat confusing. One dictum is that 'strategy is human', a seemingly redundant observation.

A more manageable approach recognises that strategy is a plan for the future, one which incorporates ends, ways and means. It is the quality of those plans, against just seven dimensions, that distinguishes strategy from an administrative approach. It is also about how strategic decisions about ends, ways and means are dependent on the choices and actions of others in the political system and are also reached in the light of experience and a changing environment. It is these criteria make strategy such an intriguing and fascinating subject.

STRATEGY DEFINED

Strategy is about planning for the future, about how any polity uses its incumbent resources (people, process and hardware and those they can develop) to achieve their long-term goals.

It is about reconciling (internally and with outside actors) ends, ways and means.

Any strategic approach must incorporate political imagination and an anticipation of competitive moves. It is therefore dynamic and contingent. Strategy is manifest in plans and processes, but the crucial dimension is that those involved think strategically.

Since there are inevitable trades-offs between ends, ways and means, *negotiating* might be a more practical word than *reconciling*, as the keepers of the political ends are not the executors of the ways or the suppliers of the means. In the next chapter, *Civil–Military Relations and Governance*, we discuss the interface between the political establishment, who define the ends, and the military, who advise and agree on ways. Both would be involved in defining means. So, both in the planning for any military venture, and in the day-to-day management, strategy is also a protocol, a series of procedures and processes, carefully monitored at every stage and advised at each stage by the appropriate experts.

STRATEGY IN PRACTICE

How then, do we actually 'do' strategy? How does it work? What does a strategic process look like? First, there must a common understanding of *what strategy is*, and the knowledge and skills to define, disseminate and implement it. Strategy must not be confused with tactics, doctrine or operational art, and although any strategy must be manifest in a plan, this plan must not inhibit future thinking; strategy is also contingent. There must be an *expectation* that strategy will be worked up, agreed and disseminated. If this seems banal, see observations to come on the Chilcot Report: *Ships in the Night*. There must also be a *forum* where strategy will be discussed, agreed and disseminated; a sofa is inadequate.

Most of all, strategy is about *action*: what are you going to do to achieve the ends? In the example above, the strategy for re-taking the Falklands could have been blockading of Argentinian ports, bombing Buenos Aires, destroying the Argentinian fleet, threatening a run on the Argentinian peso, etc. Lest the last of those sounds fanciful, during the Suez Crisis in 1956, President Eisenhower threatened Britain with a run on the pound and actually harassed the Royal Navy in the Mediterranean.

Good strategy and good strategic planning must then incorporate the seven dimensions; each forms part of the whole within the process of strategic planning and neglecting one dimension not only compromises the process itself but the quality of the output. All dimensions require clear, objective analysis and should avoid both extrapolation from the past and fashionable causes. The seven dimensions are: Political Imagination; Long-term Thinking; Competition; Environmental Sensitivity; a Multifunctional Approach; People; and Process.

POLITICAL IMAGINATION

All social and military organisations should have a sense of purpose. All organisations, military included, have inputs, outputs, and add value

Strategy does not just happen in operations rooms, in comfortable conditions: peering into the distance - a sentry, Cheshire Regiment, Somme, 1916

through management, technology and a focus on their outputs, mostly the stakeholders. Yet many organisations get their *sense of purpose and strategy* confused. *Doctrine*, a term beloved by the military, which refers to the broad principles by which armed forces shape their organisation and their actions, is a preoccupation, although a modern meme is 'operational art'. The problem is that many military organisations see doctrine or operational art as their *strategy*. Witness reports of a 'counter-insurgency strategy' from recent military campaigns. No, counter-insurgency is a tactic, maybe part of operational art, not a strategy, which involves identifying and working towards an *end*.

In his excellent 2006 article *The Lost Meaning of Strategy*, Hew Strachan, one-time Chichele Professor of the History of War at Oxford University, laments this confusion: '... risks are made greater by using terms which are not precise. Strategy clearly now embraces many more aspects than the use of military force. This meaning has migrated away from the original and there can be – and there should be – no going back ...'

In international relations, a state can have many more options than military force: sanctions; defence diplomacy or embargoes; trade deals or tariffs; leaving well alone. (See Chapter 11: The Future for War.) Strategy should not automatically involve military power. Recall the old saw, variously attributed: *If all you've got is a hammer, every problem looks like a nail.*

A strategic actor must recognise their own political sense of purpose and values but also those of the opponent, and thus gain an understanding of their value systems and preferences. This is as important as the other rules but it is one area where many campaigns become unstuck. It is essential that an opponent's reactions are anticipated, and so it needs to be understood how these decisions are made. One of the Americans' problems during the Vietnam War is that they did not understand Vietnamese culture and underestimated the North Vietnamese determination to prevail.

Similarly, during the 'Quit India' campaign during the 1930s, Mahatma Gandhi knew that he could only get away with his non-violent stance, such as having people lie down on railway tracks, on the basis that the British rulers would not use lethal force. Imagine, for a moment if India had been run by the Nazis: they would simply have murdered as many Indians as it took to achieve 'peace'. Recall the indigenous people of South-West Africa, now Namibia, where the Germans caused the deaths of up to 100,000 Hereros, Nama and San people in the early years of the twentieth century.

Strategists must beware the assumption of rationality. In short, this means that an opponent will act according to their own definition of rationality, rather than yours. They will wish to further their own ends, not yours. Insurgent groups and terrorists using women and children as human shields, something we hope the West would avoid, would illustrate this.

LONG-TERM THINKING

Strategy concerns the future. What might seem to be a rather obvious assertion is necessary because it seems part of the British character to be rather surprised by events. This raises the immediate question of how long into the future? It would be very easy to dismiss such a question with 'how long do you need?' But there are several guidelines that can be used. How long depends on two factors: how far we can look into the future and with what accuracy; how long it might take to change. At the moment the MOD publishes an excellent volume called *Global Strategic Trends*, which outlines prognoses of, for example, global health, climate change, urbanisation out to the middle of the century. This analysis is led by the MOD, the FCO and DFID with other ministries contributing. Transforming the military can take decades and, despite the Army making considerable progress over the past few years, some serving Army Officers still talk of the 'permafrost' of the military community. Another illustration might be medical: the recent COVID-19 pandemic could indicate the need for more doctors. From the moment a school-leaver opts to read medicine to becoming a GP or a hospital consultant might take up to twenty years – long-term thinking indeed.

COMPETITION

Engaging with the military community on the subject of competition would invoke surprise, tinged with a little exasperation. Of course, they would say, was it not Clausewitz himself who spoke of war being nothing more than a duel? Are we not always thinking about other states or sub-state groups, other ideologies, or competing militaries? Well yes, but the political – military process is also an open system, where competitive posture and anticipated competitive moves are as important as internal machinations. Competition here includes other ideologies and other political systems as much as other armed forces. Strategy, and to some extent policy, is contingent: everybody's strategy depends on everybody else's. Strategy is a bit like a barrel of billiard balls; move one and the rest shuffle around a bit. That is to say, everybody else's strategy has to change. It is far from clear that the US State Department always follows this.

One of the most frequent objections to strategic planning is that, as the future is uncertain, there's no point in making any plans. Indeed, former boxer Mike Tyson is often quoted as saying that 'everyone has a plan until they get punched in the mouth'. Military people in particular are fond of saying that 'no plan survives contact with the enemy'. But there is more excuse here than rationale: if you get into the ring with Mike Tyson, you might reasonably expect and even anticipate being punched in the mouth. If you want to take any military adventure, you might reasonably anticipate that there will be an enemy with their own views on things. Such objections are nugatory and display an ignorance of what strategy and the strategic process is. Strategy is always contingent.

Sifting through a variety of documents, such as speeches on foreign policy, the Strategic Defence and Security Review, the Public Accounts Scrutiny Committee report entitled *Who Does UK Strategy?* and MOD publications on doctrine reveals a recognition of competition (ideologies, cultures, enemies), but little in the way of detailed analysis, or anticipated competitive moves. Neither does there seem to be a recognition of the need to develop an analytical resource capable of assessing and anticipating the cultural, political and military posture of competing states and sub-state groups. Such resources might also be tasked with anticipating future trends.

ENVIRONMENTAL SENSITIVITY

The political–strategic military process is an open system, one where outside influences are as important as internal deliberations. Competition is a clear focus here, but there are many other influences on political–strategic choices. Without ignoring the obvious ecological considerations, let's look at just three: technology, the social environment, and the media.

TECHNOLOGICAL ADVANCES are frequently imagined to transform war and many did and do indeed take warfare, and thus war, into another dimension. Yet, most technology gets countered one way or another. Cyber war and space war are good examples. Nuclear war seems like an example where countering a nuclear attack seems impossible and ultimately pointless. Yet that assumes that any nuclear exchange will lead to nuclear escalation and the end of the world. This is not necessarily the case. Russia, for example, has developed battlefield nuclear weapons and, so reports say, may have few inhibitions about using them in conjunction with conventional weapons. In short, technology will always influence war but not determine it. This is covered in detail in Chapter 9.

THE SOCIAL ENVIRONMENT

It would be a truism to say that the strategic process is a reflection of the social environment which produces it; so much is obvious. Yet it seems to have come as something of a surprise that Britain's invasion of Iraq, and to some extent Afghanistan, did not go down too well with the British Muslim community. But, in the case of a counter-insurgency campaign, there seems to be even less analysis or effort to understand the social and cultural framework of the people among whom war is being waged. In Afghanistan, the shift from a conventional counter-insurgency campaign (what's that?) to a 'hearts and minds' campaign (what else?), while entirely appropriate, left some observers flabbergasted. It did not seem to be accompanied by any more detailed analysis or assessment of Afghanistan society or culture. The population of Afghanistan seems to have been treated as an inert part of the system, neither reactive nor, it must be said, politically aware.

THE MEDIA

The modern strategic process takes account of 24-hour rolling news; of ministers, civil servants leaking to the press; military spokesman being 'on message'; of the instant rebuttal. 'Strategic Communication' is touted as a new professional discipline. Almost any example would serve, but even a cursory juxtaposition of the government's pronouncements on Afghanistan, compared with the press media or any commentary from the 'strategic community', reveals not so much a dichotomy of views as a complete divergence. 'Strategic Communications' seems to be an unapologetic professionalisation of the party line, heavily influenced by conventional wisdoms and leavened by tabloid terror. The subsystem involving the media and press officers is regressive, with objective reality disappearing into a vortex of spin from the press office and sensationalism from the media.

A MULTIFUNCTIONAL APPROACH

Most strategic commentary focuses on the external actions taken by the organisation, using a standard set of words like *initiative, focus* or *rationalise*, often without any more precise definition or explanation. What is often forgotten is that every part and every function of the organisation should be congruent with the organisation's sense of purpose, its goal. Military organisations are usually quite good at logistical supply but pay less attention to supportive functions like Human Relations Management or language training. At one early stage in the deployment to Afghanistan, it was said there was only a handful of fluent Pashto speakers in the International Security Assistance Force HQ. Regarding IT, there are numerous articles on government failings on big IT projects. It is the least glamorous part of any strategy, but absolutely vital for success.

PEOPLE AND STRATEGIC PERSPECTIVE

Obviously, all organisations, military or political, require well-educated, experienced and mature people to generate and implement good strategy. But where will they come from and how can they be developed? Many organisations ask the question: *can strategy be taught?* So here is the definitive answer, based on many years of doing just that. You can teach strategy – reading this chapter is a good start – but it won't take you as far as you need. What you can do is to encourage managers, military officers and, dare I say, politicians to think and act more strategically. This requires a major investment in time, coaching, case studies and senior management involvement. It is beyond the scope of this book to expand on this.

PROCESS

In terms of process, there must be a respected process and forum where both strategic decisions and most of all contingent decisions can be taken and disseminated. This is covered in part in the next chapter: *Civil–Military Relations and Governance.*

FINALLY ...

Each one of the seven dimensions of strategy interacts with each other; each is as important as any other; each must be recognised as an important contribution to the generation and implementation of strategy. Ignoring any one of them will ruin the whole. The *ends, ways, means* model is not a one-time starter concept whose imperative fades. In reality it should be a dynamic model where each factor interacts with the others intrinsically and over time. *Dynamic* here is used not in its demotic sense of 'exciting' but in its classic sense of moving, in that each factor influences the other. The time factor is vital. Ends shift with changing political circumstances, practical experience and other exogenous factors; ways develop and improve; and means may be augmented by other, new resources and may also be developed internally. Thus, as well as understanding what strategy is, decision makers need to think more strategically continuously.

Note also that we do not mention military action *per se*. Modern strategy should be about much more than the use of armed force. We cover this fully in Chapter 11, The Future for War. Even when Clausewitz was writing his tome, *ways* included diplomacy, military pre-emption, offensive kinetic action (bang bang) or simply bludgeoning the enemy until he listened, as the end of the Second World War will attest.

HOW WELL, THEN, DOES BRITAIN DO STRATEGY?

Not well. There is a perennial air of resignation about academic and think-tank writing on the subject. Witness articles such as *British National Strategy: Who Does It?* (2013) by Hew Strachan, who asserted that 'the term *strategy* has acquired a universality which has robbed it of meaning,' or *Why Britain Doesn't Do Grand Strategy* (2010) by Patrick Porter, an Australian/British academic, or *Strategy? No Thanks, We're British* (2013) by Richard Norton-Taylor, a British journalist.

But all is not lost! Parliament is on the case! In October 2010 (there's been very little since then), the House of Commons Public Administration Select Committee published a report of their deliberations on *Who Does UK National Strategy?* It was timely: in numerous articles over the years, academics, civil servants, military personnel and think-tankers have lamented either *The Lost Meaning of Strategy* (Hew Strachan again) or that governments of whatever hue seemed to have lost an institutionalised capacity for and culture of strategic thought (Sir Jock Stirrup, RAF, one-time Chief of the Defence Staff).

The committee interviewed civil servants, military officers and the Foreign Secretary. It took written evidence from experts and think-tank professors but only one from a UK university (the London School of Economics). Notably absent was anybody from King's College London War Studies Department (the country's leading repository of thinking about war), the International Institute for Strategic Studies (ditto Strategic Studies) or The Royal United Services Institute (ditto the military).

The committee recognised that strategy is a ubiquitous term ... *that has lost its precision and become detached from its original military meaning.* But its answer to the question *Who Does UK National Strategy?* was simple: no one. Its solution was that the then recently established National Security Council and the post of National Security Advisor should have their remit widened to encompass National Strategy with a *central coordinating role.* This might prove a bit tricky if you weren't sure what strategy was in the first place, but the committee also suggested establishing a *community of strategists,* and that to foster such a community, government would need to look at its recruitment practices.

They got a bit closer when they looked ... *into the capacity we have as a country to devise and sustain a continuing process which can promote our national interest* ... but shuffled that off to the National Security Council. Although implied, there was no specific mention that the strategic protocols, procedures and processes were not adequate to the task.

That same year, 2010, the *RUSI Journal* published an article: *Reclaiming the Art of British Strategic Thinking,* by Major General Paul Newton, Air Vice-Marshal Paul Colley and Brigadier Andrew Sharpe, all people with, one would suppose, considerable experience of defining or at least advising on strategy. They bemoaned the fact that Britain lacked any 'Grand Strategic Manifesto', due to what they suspected was 'intellectual decay' and the absence of easily recognisable and accessible bodies of professional knowledge. They also blamed too great a focus on doctrine and tactics and a more recent preoccupation with 'operational art'. Nowhere did they attempt to define what they meant by a *Grand Strategic Manifesto* or how it would support strategic thinking. Neither did they define *strategy* or the necessary process for it or how they envisaged people could think strategically.

They quoted some historical examples of 'grand strategy' but failed to draw the right conclusions. It was not so much Wellington's success at Waterloo in 1815 that achieved a strategic outcome but the allied coalition, carefully assembled and financed over the years by the British government. Cannae in 216 BC was indeed a tactical success for Hannibal against the Romans but the strategic failure came from Carthage, not from one of the greatest generals the world has known. They were, however, right about Pharsalus in 48 BC, in that it provided a strategic decision, but they failed to spot the important fact that the policy, grand strategy, doctrine and tactics were all in the hands of one brilliant military man: Gaius Julius Caesar.

They went on to suggest that: 'The armed forces have an intellectual and constitutional obligation to inform, persuade and even encourage our civil leadership to engage in a strategic dialogue'. Furthermore, that 'The ways and the means have become a substitute for strategic analysis and discourse on achieving the ends.' And that 'operations' had taken over from thinking about strategy. Their examples confirmed the poverty of thinking in the British military today. Since they are all one-star generals and above, one is bound to ask of them: what exactly were you doing, general, when you took the Queen's shilling?

The *Who Does UK National Strategy* report and *Reclaiming the Art of British Strategic Thinking* are, together, a useful recognition of the deficiencies in Britain's approach to strategy and for that alone they might be praised. Some of the solutions suggested are a mixture of the usual suspects, some just apple pie and aspiration. But neither recognise the scope of *strategy* and what Britain has by way of intellectual resource. There is a thriving and vibrant strategic community within the country, represented by various think-tanks (IISS, Chatham House, RUSI) and various universities. When the author asked a senior academic about why the government did not consult more widely, his response was immediate: 'they don't always ask us, but if they do, it's always too late.' As the man in the pub observed, 'nuf said'.

7. CIVIL-MILITARY RELATIONS AND GOVERNANCE

INTRODUCTION

'You do the fighting and I'll do the talking,' was the admonition – jibe even – delivered to senior military figures during the NATO-led (well, Britain and France) military intervention in Libya in 2011. David Richards, the UK Chief of the Defence Staff from 2009 to 2013, had had several 'bruising encounters' with the then Prime Minister, David Cameron, as recorded in Richards' biography *Taking Command*. Richards explained that, in bombing Libya, he could only 'make space for a political settlement', a framework for the politicians (that is to say local politicians with international help) to work out a political solution. *War is a political act* ... What Richards couldn't do was to provide the political solution itself, hence Cameron's comment about 'I'll do the talking'. He didn't.

CIVIL-MILITARY RELATIONS

The Libyan adventure is an intriguing insight into the relationship between the executive government and the military. This is known as Civil–Military Relations (CMR), a subject that generates little or no attention from the general public. Civil–Military Relations has been a concern of statesmen ever since there were discernible polities. It is mentioned in Plato's *Republic*, Machiavelli addressed the issue and one can see its failure in the German approach to World War I and in the stresses between the Allies in World War II.

Civil–Military Relations concerns the relationship between civil society and the military established to provide their physical security. In particular, Civil–Military Relations focuses on the subordinate position

Soldiers must feel they are part of the society that sends them out to risk life and limb. Most politicians visit soldiers in the field, mainly for the coverage in the press the next day

of the military to the legitimate government. Civilian control is actually government control, even though the government is democratically elected or at least legitimate. In short, the government gives the orders and the military obeys. As David Richards himself once said, 'I'm a soldier, so ultimately I do as I'm told.' This is true, but only up to a point; a soldier must in general obey a legal command, but if that command is not legal, he may refuse. This strays into the area of military law, which is detailed and complex. CMR is important because ...

LIBYA

The Libyan venture, Operation Unified Protector, involved enforcing a no-fly zone across Libya and, supposedly, the interdiction of any Libyan forces threatening the civilian population. Thus, the operation was ostensibly an exercise to protect civilians but subsequent revelations (and the suspicion at the time) indicate that the real rationale, certainly for the Americans but probably also for the British and French, was the overthrow of Gaddafi and 'regime change'.

In the event, the military 'did the fighting', though not quite as much as was claimed. Libya descended into factionalism and warlordism, a situation that continues to this day. The subsequent House of Commons Foreign Affairs Committee Report (*HC 119*, published September 2016) concluded that:

This policy was not informed by accurate intelligence. (Though plenty must have been available.) *In particular, the government failed to identify that the threat to civilians was overstated and that the rebels included a significant Islamist element. By the summer of 2011, the limited intervention to protect civilians had drifted into an opportunist policy of regime change.* (Who did the 'drifting'? Politicians or the military?) *That policy was not underpinned by a strategy to support and shape post-Gaddafi Libya. The result was political and economic collapse, inter-militia and inter-tribal warfare, humanitarian, and migrant crises, widespread human rights violations, the spread of Gaddafi regime weapons across the region and the growth of ISIL in North Africa. Through his decision making in the National Security Council, former Prime Minister David Cameron was ultimately responsible for the failure to develop a coherent Libya strategy.*

So, we can hardly conclude that Cameron 'did the talking'. Incidentally, the British intervention alone is reckoned to have cost the British taxpayer about £1bn, and this during the time of supposed 'austerity'. Also, one might have thought that lessons had been learned after the experience of Afghanistan and Iraq. This episode suggests that there are not only some conceptual gaps in thinking about Civil–Military Relations but also serious organisational and cultural gaps, not generally addressed. There are three aspects to CMR: the relationship between the legitimate government of the day and the military; the relationship between the military and society in general; and the somewhat dreary but vital subject of governance. Also, we need to recognise the other influences on the use of military power: the legislature, the judiciary and, with much more impact, the civil service.

Governance is the key, and of fundamental importance when considering military action. There is also the concept of *Strategic Culture*, which is often taken as a proxy for governance. To put it all more starkly, good governance would have made Chilcot and one or two other reports unnecessary. Indeed, one might even say that with good governance, the Libyan adventure (make that Iraq and Afghanistan as well) might not have happened at all.

THE RISKS OF A MILITARY COUP

One problem for any civil power is how to make the military strong enough to do its job while not posing the threat of interference in politics or, ultimately, a military coup. Lest the prospect of a military coup – certainly in Europe – sounds remote, since the Second World War there was a danger of a military coup in France in 1961 (post-Algeria), an actual coup in Greece ('The Colonels') in 1967, and attempts in Spain in 1978, 1981, 1982 and 1985. There may even have been a military coup in Italy but no one noticed as it was lunchtime.

In Britain, the 1968 plot (not necessarily military) against Harold Wilson could be put down to silliness. The 1974 (one has to say *alleged*) British coup against Wilson and Jim Callaghan (allegedly they were Soviet agents) seems more credible, though the hard evidence concerns the MI5 bugging of Downing Street rather than a military effort.

THEORY?

There is a small canon of literature about Civil–Military Relations in the US, but little on the subject in the United Kingdom, and British academics and think-tankers generally see this subject as a secondary rather than primary interest. The prime focus over the past few years has been the Military Covenant.

There are three main concepts of CMR: the first from Samuel Huntington, an American political scientist and academic who wrote the seminal, though disputed, *The Clash of Civilizations*. His 'normal' theory envisaged 'the proper subordination of a competent, professional military to the ends of policy as determined by civilian authority'. The exemplification of this would be the idea that strategy begins where politics ends, a neat but unworkable concept and one at odds with the doyen of writers on strategy, Carl von Clausewitz. The fundamental idea is that the civilian leadership identifies the political objective of any military action, albeit with military advice, but then leaves it to the military world (that is, the officer corps) to identify and execute the best way of achieving that objective. Control over the military is exercised by the legal and constitutional arrangements and mutual respect.

ELIOT COHEN

Cohen, an American political scientist, albeit somewhat hawkish, as his *The Big Stick: The Limits of Soft Power and the Necessity of Military Force* might demonstrate, has a keen interest in CMR. In his seminal book *Supreme Command* (2002), he analyses Civil–Military Relations within the context of leadership, politics and strategy. He accepts Huntington's concept of military professionalism but suggests that the normal theory, that of civilian control, needs emendation in the light of the experiences that he chronicles. His analyses of the wartime experiences of Lincoln, Clemenceau, Churchill and Ben-Gurion are intriguing and, as it says on the cover, make it a 'great read'. But the more subtle points he makes are of vital importance. His subjects, while respecting military judgement, would unhesitatingly query, prod, probe, and nag their generals, and in many cases dismiss them, and would suggest and arbitrate on any subject they felt was important for the war effort. These ranged from major (strategic) initiatives through to small arms suitability. (Lincoln, for example, would test small arms himself. Given the lengthy delays in the British Army in selecting a new rifle, this would seem to be not a bad idea.)

Cohen concludes his comments on this subject with a chapter on *Leadership without Genius*, resisting the temptation to end on a lament that modern statesmen are nothing like those mentioned above. The lessons he advances is that '... political leaders must immerse themselves in the conduct of their wars no less than their great projects of domestic legislation ...' In short, that they must '... master their military briefs as thoroughly as they do their civilian ones. As part of this, they must demand and expect from their military subordinate candor as bruising as it is necessary ...' He then comments that both groups must expect a *running conversation* in which '... although civilian opinion will not usually dictate, it must dominate, and that the conversation will cover not only ends and policies, but ways and means.' A stark contrast to Cameron's comment above, and some vindication for General David Richards, who also advised that he – that is, the military – could only *make space for a political settlement*; they could not win the war and, incidentally (though one can be sure this was not at the back of Richards' mind, it might have been in Cameron's), enhance Cameron's reputation. The comment echoes what US General Jack Keane said after Iraq: 'I think that we, as military leaders, bend too much to national leaders but what I am challenging is our reluctance to be completely honest with them, if need be to the point of being brutal.'

There are two more points that, while rather prosaic, are of great bearing here. Servicemen and women would much prefer to be in action than resident in barracks: the Navy would prefer to be sailing, almost to the exclusion of anything else, and the RAF flying. They do not, in general, try and resist action. The experience of the US military is slightly different: on some occasions, the Pentagon has been at odds with the State Department as the military did not want to be drawn into messy, non-specific wars, preferring to fight proper wars with proper opponents. And, of course, the military urging caution on any military venture may be seen as military timidity, not welcomed by politicians.

So much for the theory. Does it help? Let us look at some recent experiences and see how CMR worked, or didn't, in some recent campaigns and, more particularly, the British Army's deployment to Iraq. The Chilcot Report provides a detailed and up-to-date account of the planning for, and to a lesser extent the conduct of, the invasion and occupation of Iraq in 2003. First, some background:

THE IRAQ WAR

The Iraq War of 2003, was a US-led coalition campaign to topple Saddam Hussein and his Ba'ath Party from power and to introduce freedom and democracy to the Iraqi people. The rationale was based on some suspicion that Saddam Hussein was developing Weapons of Mass Destruction (WMD) and, after considerable debate, the UN Security Council adopted a compromise resolution (*SC Resolution 1441* November 2002) which authorised the resumption of weapons inspections and promised 'serious consequences' for non-compliance.

However, and the point that preoccupied the British media was that *prior* to SCR 1441, Tony Blair and George W Bush had already agreed to remove Saddam Hussein from power through an invasion and military occupation of the country. It was later claimed that Blair had told Bush that the British stood 'shoulder to shoulder' with the United States on this issue and that he would be 'with you' whatever. Despite massive demonstrations across the country (*not in my name* being the tagline), Blair decided to go ahead and become a coalition partner for the invasion. This was passed by a whipped vote in Parliament.

The invasion itself, given the overwhelming airpower of the United States, was an overwhelming success but almost everything after that was a tragic failure. Such was the pressure on the British government for an enquiry, that the then Prime Minister, Gordon Brown, announced on 15 June 2009 an enquiry into the circumstances surrounding the invasion and subsequent occupation. Sir John Chilcot, a retired British civil servant, was appointed to lead the enquiry.

THE CHILCOT REPORT

The Chilcot Report covered the run-up to the conflict, the subsequent military action and its aftermath. The objective was to establish how decisions were made, to determine exactly what happened and to identify lessons to ensure that, in a similar situation in future, the British government would be equipped to respond in the most effective manner, and in the best interests of the country. It took seven years to complete and was finally published in July 2016. A ludicrous delay on such an important subject.

The eagerly awaited results achieved what the media were looking for: to 'skewer' Tony Blair. Richard Norton-Taylor (hardly unbiased) wrote in *The Guardian* that Tony Blair was 'guilty of taking the country to war before peaceful alternatives had been exhausted, undermining the authority of the UN Security Council, leaving Britain more at risk of a terror attack, and helping to provoke a conflict that led to the deaths of 179 British troops and of at least 50,000 Iraqis'. Norton-Taylor went on to say that Blair was 'allowed to make decisions by discarding all pretence at Cabinet government, subverting the intelligence agencies, and making exaggerated claims about threats to Britain's national security'. Philippe Sands, an Anglo-French QC, observed rather perceptively that the report 'pulled its punches but marshalled the factual evidence in such a way that an inference of lying, deceit or manipulation was possible'.

The Chilcott Report is something of an exhausting read; even the Executive Summary is 150 pages long. The key points, certainly with regard to Civil–Military Relations, are elusive. For example, there are 200 pages on the MOD's procurement system, but no firm conclusion about who was responsible for making sure that the right equipment was provided to the front line.

The report's main findings were four-fold, with author's comments in parentheses:

1) *The case for war was deficient* (hardly a revelation);
2) *The legal basis for war was far from satisfactory* (civil servant speak for *pretty shaky or non-existent*);
3) *The UK overestimated the ability to influence US decisions on Iraq* (ignorant, it seems, of Charles Wheeler's famous line that 'America has a special relationship with just one country – America');
4) (And the most pertinent for our purposes) *On these matters of strategy and diplomacy, the Inquiry recognises that there is no standard formula* (civil servant speak for *in the lap of the gods*);
5) *War preparation and planning was wholly inadequate* (see comment on the first finding).

Conventional wisdoms, academic and think-tank comments and popular opinion do not allow any persuasive defence of Tony Blair. He would not expect it, nor does he deserve it. Fair enough, he must shoulder the lion's share of whatever blame is appropriate. Yet one has to ask if, had events turned out differently, Tony Blair might even have been a hero of our time. Suppose Paul Bremer (Leader of the Coalition Provisional Authority in Iraq from 2003 to 2004) had *not* decided (unilaterally, it seems) to de-Ba'ath the Iraqi government, *not* to disband the Iraq army and *not* to sack thousands of teachers ... might then the occupation have been a success? Are there clues or scraps here that may be applied to our core Civil–Military Relations problematic?

First, Chilcot decided to record individuals' recollections of events. Were the minutes, notes of meetings, position papers inadequate? What? They were not comprehensive? Well, obviously not; let us blame Tony Blair. In all, Chilcot called some forty-six senior officers of general rank. That's generals, naval commodores and air commodores and above. What Chilcot does not say is that, despite this league of senior people (and this will have included the Cabinet Secretary as well as the Permanent Undersecretary at the Ministry of Defence), Tony Blair was 'allowed' to make decisions. This simply does not ring true: what were these people doing?

Second, the report was also subject to 'Maxwellisation', a process whereby persons who are to be criticised in an official report are able to respond prior to publication, based on details of the criticism received in advance. There may, therefore, have been a danger that they put their evidence in the way that reflected well upon themselves.

Third, people who gave evidence to Chilcot were not under oath, although one might imagine that any reasonably competent QC might have got a lot more out of some of them.

Fourth, there are few normative assertions along the lines of *what should have happened* or that *so-and-so should have consulted with so-and-so, in writing and communicated this down the line.* In short, there are few organisational insights identifying who was responsible for what, and when. The witness list, as is common with government reports, does not list anyone with expertise in the diagnosis or resolution of organisational problems, line of command or, more to the point, lines of responsibility.

Overall, there's very little in the Chilcot Report that we can apply to the problematic of Civil–Military Relations. It does not live up to its promise if judged against its purpose of *identifying lessons to ensure that ... the British government is equipped to respond in the most effective manner ...*

It does, however, live up to a long tradition of government reports: exhaustive, detailed, Maxwellised, ignorant of any organisational principles; welcomed by the minister (usually the one *after* the subject of the enquiry) who trots out the usual 'lessons will be learned' mantra. Then, thank goodness, things can revert to the status quo ante.

With Jesuitical humility, typical of the British civil servant, Chilcot does not see the report as the place for recommendations or even suggestions as to how things might be improved in the future, though these are implied. Yes, given the will and the capability of managing organisational change, there might be some lessons learned, but we could confidently predict that the next time something like this happens, the same problems will recur. We might expect MOD procurement still to be a complete disaster area, that the Armed Forces will not prune their top-heavy command structures and the nexus for strategy making and implementation will still be vague and obscure.

CHRISTOPHER ELLIOTT'S *HIGH COMMAND*

A more up-to-date commentary on Civil–Military Relations is well observed in a book published in 2015 by Major General Christopher L. Elliott, entitled *High Command: British Military Leadership in the Iraq and Afghanistan Wars.*

At 250 pages it cannot be summarised easily but some examples will illustrate the author's conclusions. Regarding planning for the Iraq escapade, is it really true that General Sir Michael Walker, Chief of the Defence Staff (CDS) in May 2003, *felt certain* that all important decisions had been discussed thoroughly at the Chief of Staff's committee? He only 'felt'? Were there no minutes? It gets worse: his Chief of the General Staff, Head of the Army, General Mike Jackson said that he did not know enough of what was going on: 'I often learned about things after they had been decided and I often didn't know where a decision had been made ... but orders were orders so you just got on with it.' In fact, it's part of the more general pattern: without quoting chapter and verse, on some occasions we have the CJO (Chief of Joint Operations) back at PJHQ (Permanent Joint Headquarters) making decisions, sometimes CDS making decisions, sometimes the MoD delegating matters to the commander on the ground while, at the same time, those on the ground were complaining of gross interference in the day-to-day minutiae of tactical operations. This was made worse by direction coming from staff offices in PJHQ Northwood, many of whom were from the RAF and Navy, who had very limited or non-existent experience of land operations.

Overall strategy? Christopher Elliott concludes that sometimes there were three conflicting strategies about Iraq running at the same time: in the Iraq theatre, in the British MOD, and in the Prime Minister's office in 10 Downing Street. General Sir Robert Fry would say later, 'Grand strategy or policy and strategy passed as ships in the night. None was particularly strategic.'

At one stage, British troops were 'drawn down' from Iraq and sent to Afghanistan, and the story gets even more bizarre. In an interview in June 2010 with journalist Deborah Haynes of *The Times*, Mike Jackson, Head of the Army at the time, was asked why the Army was deployed to Helmand province in Afghanistan rather than Kandahar. Mike Jackson replied, '*Search me, guv.*' Was he really saying that he had no idea why his assets had been deployed as they were? It is simply staggering.

Elliott comments on why things went wrong and asks whether the current arrangements are 'fit for the future'. Though he does not quite spell it out, the answer seems to be a resounding *no*. He critiques the background, training and education of any future CDS, suggesting that, like their American counterparts, they do a six to twelve month attachment to the university, to think about ... *strategy*, giving strategy a profile in the military world that simply does not exist at the moment. Lest Elliott's views seem too partisan, more testimony comes from various commentaries on the British Army in Basra, southern Iraq, and from those intimately involved in *Operation Charge of the Knights*.

BASRA (SOUTHERN IRAQ)

A full account of the British Army's six-year tenure in Basra would be lengthy, but suffice to say that the outlines are clear. *Operation Sinbad*, starting in September 2006, was, to quote from an article in *the RUSI Journal* by Colonel Richard Iron, 'The Charge of the Knights', a 'true counter-insurgency campaign'. If the Iraq escapade was a failure, Basra was a disaster. Taken with some observations from Chilcot and Elliott, we might formulate nine key questions.

1) In what type of conflict were we engaged in Iraq? Counter-insurgency? Policing? Much of the 'insurgent' activity in Basra was simply criminal. Peacekeeping? Conventional war? It was not clear, then or now. Clausewitz said famously: 'No one starts a war – or rather, no one in his senses ought to do so – without first being clear in his mind what he intends to achieve by that war and how he intends to conduct it.'

2) Did we develop a strategy (systems, processes, procedures) for engagement with the US? Having fought so much alongside them in the past, and the Prime Minister saying that he would stand 'shoulder to shoulder' with the US, whatever – it hardly looks like it.

3) Did we understand the importance and role of indigenous militias and our relationship with them? There were both Sunni insurgents and Iran-backed Shia groups. One might ask what the intelligence people were doing.

4) To what extent did we interdict insurgents and support from Iran? Again, what were the intelligence people doing?

5) What about civil development in the counter-insurgency campaign? Reports suggested that projects started under one commander were arbitrarily abandoned by the next, six months later. What were all the NGOs doing? Was there no coordination? Was there no ... you know ... plan?

6) Did we have the right people for the job and train them properly, despite the enormous value that the Armed Forces quite rightly puts on training? Perhaps senior officers think they know it all and don't need any CPD – Continuing Professional Development, as it's called in the commercial sector. And, most of all, where was the political input?

7) Who was making decisions about Basra? Come to think about it, who was making decisions about Iraq? Local commanders? Nouri al-Maliki? Politicians in Whitehall? The MoD? The Americans? CDS? PJHQ?

And, not surprisingly:

8) It seems there was no strategy for Basra so the effort there was never resourced for success.

And finally, from Iron's testimony:

9) Six-month command tours were the single greatest cause of military failure. (That is, of the senior officer in Iraq.) So, no continuity and little coordination, a practice totally within the responsibility of senior generals to change.)

LESSONS FROM BASRA

Some of these (development, six-month tours, who was making decisions?) are simple, if laborious to adopt; others, such as the type of war, strategy, and working with coalition partners are more fundamental.

There is very little evidence anywhere to suggest that the government is addressing these factors generally or specifically. Given several, if not many, undefined and maybe unknown threats, it is a matter of the utmost urgency. The security of the Unite Kingdom depends on it.

THE MILITARY COVENANT

Rather too much commentary views Civil–Military Relations simply through the prism of the Military Covenant. Notwithstanding that a bond of mutual obligations has existed between the British state and its Armed Forces going back generations, the British Army chose to open the new millennium with a doctrinal statement that has become known as the *Military Covenant*. Published in 2000, it was generally thought to be a great step forward. It's quite short, so is reproduced here in full:

The Military Covenant is the mutual obligation between the Nation, the Army and each individual soldier; an unbreakable common bond of identity, loyalty and responsibility which has sustained the Army throughout its history. Soldiers will be called upon to make personal sacrifices – including the ultimate sacrifice – in the service of the Nation. In putting the needs of the Nation and the Army before their own, they forego some of the rights enjoyed by those outside the Armed Forces. In return, British soldiers must always be able to expect fair treatment, to be valued and respected as individuals, and that they (and their families) will be sustained and rewarded by commensurate terms and conditions of service.

It attracted some, but not universal coverage, though it does not specifically cover sailors or airmen; or those involved in the back areas. (*'They also serve who only stand and wait'*. – Milton). The institution of the Military Covenant was and remains invaluable, but it does little to resolve the core Civil–Military Relations challenge.

PARLIAMENTARY SCRUTINY

The government's focus has moved on, rather slowly, to parliamentary scrutiny and control. In 2007, the UK government published a consultation paper entitled *The Governance of Britain: War powers and treaties: limiting Executive Powers*. In it, it was recognised that *The power to ... send armed forces into conflict situations ... is the most important power a government can wield. But there is presently no legal requirement for the ... the House of Commons ... to have any particular role ...* In practice, it suggests that *no government these days would seek to commit troops to a substantial overseas deployment without giving Parliament the opportunity to debate it.* It admits that *... it has been rare in the past for Parliament to have a substantive vote on a proposed deployment before the troops are committed.* Progress since then has been slow, according to Philippe Lagassé of the Norman Paterson School of International Affairs, Carleton University, Ottawa, Canada:

... despite sustained calls to displace the war prerogative, however, the legal authority to deploy armed forces remains with the executive, with a convention of political control layered atop it. The British government has blocked attempts to displace the war prerogative in law, owing to the risk of judicial review ... However, sustained pressure from backbenchers and parliamentary committees meant that the war prerogative could not be left entirely unaffected ... This has led to the layering compromise: a convention of parliamentary control would be formed, giving the Commons an informal veto over major military deployments involving combat ... continuing calls for a displacement of the war prerogative are unlikely to succeed unless a statute can provide an equal degree of flexibility and protection from judicial review.

What is wrong, one might ask, with the idea of a judicial review? No one would dispute that the government – any government – must retain the right and responsibility to act immediately without parliamentary approval should the urgent need arise from an immediate threat to the integrity of the United Kingdom. The above system is, for the UK, about as good as we're going to get, and can be reckoned *adequate* if not perfect. The author's preference would be that any deployment of British troops should be put to Parliament with an un-whipped vote, and this should be confirmed every six months.

COMMENTARY

Using military force is the most potent action that any government can take. Military ventures cost an enormous amount of money, and military hardware inflation costs always seem to be higher than general inflation and, given the increasingly technical aspects of war, training costs escalate in a similar way. Foreign wars, even peace-oriented, also cost considerable political capital, both domestic and international, particularly if not successful, and their legacy can be very long-lived – remember Suez.

Most of all, though, they cost lives, both of the domestic population and the target country. For better or worse, British military deaths since the end of the Second World War have been over 5,000. Military and civilian deaths as a result of the Iraq invasion are difficult to identify. The Watson Institute of Brown University say that more than 182,000 Iraqi civilians were killed between 2003 and 2018 by direct violence. Actual figures are thought to be much higher and many quotes are somewhere between 460,000 and 655,000, a significant proportion of the Iraqi population. For Afghanistan, it's even more difficult to identify, but 200,000 would seem a reasonable estimate.

Using military force is a heavy responsibility and one that should be subject to intense scrutiny, before, during and after deployment. Civil–Military Relations theory did not help in the above wars and there are significant weaknesses. First, it has moved on only very slowly, in any practical sense, since the establishment of the notion of military subordination to civil power. Second is timescale. There are three distinct modes in military operations: force structure and procurement (long-term); campaign planning (pre-deployment) and day-to-day operations management (during deployment). The generals and the civil servants who plan force structure and procurement are not those who will have to live with the consequences. There is little in current Civil–Military Relations commentaries that recognises this.

So instead of treating Civil–Military Relations as a mongrel academic subject, one rooted in 'custom and practice', it needs to be relocated as a *governance* issue, one rooted in organisational and strategic theory, with reference to psychology, sociology, anthropology and political science.

Deliberations about war, or just the use of military force, should involve many parties: the government, Parliament, the civil service, the judiciary and the military, as well as the views of any relevant think-tank, academic or even NGO. At the moment, certainly in the UK, they don't. It would seem unrealistic to suggest that each party should be thoroughly informed of the social and political situation of the enemy and the capabilities and implications of the deployment. Yet often this does not appear to be the case: decisions seem to be made in an arbitrary manner, to such an extent that some commentators even talk about Britain 'muddling through' (albeit with 'smart' as a qualifier) with regard to military deployments and foreign adventures.

War must be about changing the balance between polities and about both domestic and international politics. With military action, we need to consider the other side's politics as well as our own. And that needs to draw a distinction here between an *enemy*, being an insurgent group, and an *opposition*, being a resentful local population.

A broader, governance-based approach, one grounded in organ-isational and strategic theory would encompass the evolution and implementation of strategy, define the protocols to be used and take account of the need for political intercourse.

CONCLUSIONS: GOOD GOVERNANCE

What, then, is good governance and how does this relate and contribute to Civil–Military Relations and, in particular, the use of military force? The meaning of *governance* is not so much disputed as disparate: there are as many definitions as there are applications. But let's not get carried away with definitions; good governance is a system of information flows and of checks and balances and fits well into the protocols of the strategic process. Good governance provides *accountability*, to co-locate authority and responsibility; *controls* to facilitate *control* (controls do not necessarily give you control: think of a racing car), and it demands a *responsible expectation and commitment* to the process and also, importantly, a *forum*. Overall, governance is *purposeful* and is focused on outcomes. As such, governance accords with Clausewitz's dicta and, taken together with the other factors, ensures that the political outcomes are not neglected.

8. LEGITIMATE OR ILLEGITIMATE WAR?

The 2003 coalition invasion of Iraq is outlined in Chapter 7, Civil–Military Relations and Governance, pp 101–102, and has been the subject of fierce controversy ever since. Here, we are not concerned specifically with the dispute over the interpretation of the UN Security Council Resolution or the claim that Saddam Hussein possessed Weapons of Mass Destruction. It is certainly clear that this was exaggerated both by the Secretary of State Colin Powell in Washington and by Prime Minister Tony Blair in London. In particular, Tony Blair claimed that Saddam Hussein could launch a WMD attack in forty-five minutes. The allegation is that Blair, or at least those reporting to him had 'sexed up' the dossier to oblige Parliament to back him in joining President Bush's invasion.

The question is whether the war was legal, legitimate or had any moral standing. Certainly, the word *illegal* was subsequently used by the then United Nations Secretary General Kofi Annan because the war was not sanctioned by the United Nations Security Council. On the other hand – and this illustrates the difficulty of judging these matters – Tony Blair has been persistent in defending his decision, reminding his detractors that Saddam Hussein was a criminal, practising genocide and murder on his own people and that the world was a better place for of his removal. George Bush's claim that he was 'returning' Iraq to 'freedom and democracy' can be discounted, as subsequent events will confirm. George Bush even used the rather weak argument that Saddam Hussein had tried to assassinate the former President Bush, his father, by a car bomb during Bush Sr's visit to Kuwait University in May 1993. This was an alleged 'hostile act' that was actually never realised.

This is in contrast to the 1990 invasion of Kuwait. In August 1990,

Iraqi forces invaded and occupied Kuwait. A subsequent Security Council Resolution (678) empowered states to use *all necessary means to force Iraq out of Kuwait*. A coalition was formed to do this, which commenced military operations in January 1991. This is subsequently accepted as a 'legal war', because it was sanctioned by the United Nations Security Council.

The legality, legitimacy or moral standing of war in general and of any particular war has been debated by politicians, military leaders and legal experts ever since wars started. It was recently claimed that the ancient Egyptians concerned themselves with such matters and certainly ancient Chinese and Indian civilisations did too.

What is now known as the 'just war tradition' is the result of many thinkers, philosophers and legal authorities deliberating over the centuries. The ancient Greeks were not ambivalent about war, seeing it as a necessary evil and often lamenting the pain and destruction it caused. The claim in Chapter 1, War in History: The Persistence of War, that the Greeks 'had a go at ... well, anyone' may be something of an exaggeration, but any history of that period seems, from a modern perspective, to be one of endless wars. Aristotle took an ethical approach to war, and thought that war should always be fought for the sake of peace, and then only as a last resort. He justified self-defence but accepted that an ethical war could be fought for the acquisition of resources or, horrifically to modern sensibilities, for the enslavement of an inferior (that is, non-Greek) people. In fact, many wars were fought for the acquisition of resources, including slaves, and particularly women to bear more of the victor's children. Plato wrote a little about war; his main concern being that the rightful conduct of war was linked to the practice of virtue and justice. For Plato, good law should engender peace, not war, and he also recognised the importance of legitimate authority in war-making.

The Romans had a concept of a 'just cause' for war, sometimes their allegation that a treaty between Rome and another state had been broken, but the object of the justice was not the hapless enemy, but the gods, intermediated by the priests. Otherwise, they concerned themselves mainly with the internal legal procedures of war, undertaking elaborate ceremonies of speeches and the throwing of spears into enemy territory. (The gods, of course, are still with us, but now we call them money, power and face.) Of course, resources were also important to the Romans, including slaves. *The Rape of the Sabine Women* is a famous painting by Peter Paul Rubens, and illustrates this aspect of war. Although now thought of as mythological, the rape is actually a poor translation of the Latin *raptio*, meaning abduction. It seems that, shortly after it was founded in the mid-eighth century BC, Rome was populated by fugitive men and bandits. At a festival, the Roman men seized some of the Sabine women and fought off the Sabine men. The one non-virgin captured was said to have married Romulus. Interestingly from the feminist point of view, it was she, Hersilia, who subsequently intervened to stop a war between the Romans and the Sabines.

For the Western world, Christianity had a major impact on thinking about the legitimacy, morality and legality of war. The summary term is *justice* and the narrative is now 'just war'. One of the most well-known books on this is Michael Walzer's *Just and Unjust Wars*. Christian thinking about war developed over the years. Some of the principles survived to the present day; some have been modified, some disappeared. Saint Augustine of Hippo (now north eastern Algeria) was a Roman citizen who lived from AD 354 to 430 in the twilight of the western Roman Empire. He influenced Western philosophy and Christianity and his seminal work, *The City of God*, has given its name to a modern film. Starting from a Christian viewpoint, Augustine tried to reconcile the obligation of Roman citizens to go to war for Rome when required, with a pacifist, 'turn the other cheek' viewpoint. Given that the Roman Empire was in the process of splitting into eastern (Constantinople) and western (Rome) regions and was subject to external pressure from what the Romans called barbarians, this presented a major political challenge. His famous dictum was:

We do not seek peace in order to be at war, but we go to war that we may have peace. Be peaceful, therefore, in warring, so that you may vanquish those whom you war against, and bring them to the prosperity of peace.

He also asserted that rulers had a duty to maintain peace and that this gave them the right to fight wars in order to keep the peace.

Thomas Aquinas (1225 to 1274), was an Italian philosopher and theologian. He developed the ideas of Aristotle, Plato and Saint Augustine, and advanced a set of criteria for a 'just war'. this depiction by Louis Figuier, 1881

Saint Thomas Aquinas, who lived from 1225 to 1274, was an Italian Dominican friar, philosopher and theologian. He developed the ideas of Aristotle, Plato and Saint Augustine. Aquinas advanced a set of criteria for a 'just war'. First, any war had to be initiated by a rightful sovereign, described as a leader who had the welfare of his subjects at heart and one who operated within the law. (Aquinas' doctrine was a set of theological Christian rules rather than a system of international law. It was not until the fifteenth century that the notion of a secular international law emerged.) To all intents and purposes, this meant the sovereign, *provided* he (it was usually a 'he') was a good king, legitimately established. Second, any war had to be waged for a 'just cause', on account of some wrong the kingdom had suffered from the action of another. Third, there had to be the intent to promote good and avoid evil. Finally, violence was only justified to the extent it was necessary.

Hugo Grotius was a Dutch humanist, lawyer and theologian who lived from 1583 to 1645. Involved in the intra-Calvinist disputes of the Dutch Republic, he wrote most of his major works in exile in France. He is famous for the foundations for international law, based on Protestant concepts of natural law. He is remembered for two influential works germane to our enquiries: *The Free Seas* and *On the Law of War and Peace.* The latter still has resonance today. It was a prodigious attempt to build some broad moral consensus into considerations of war. He wrote:

... there is a common law among nations, which is valid alike for war and in war ... throughout the Christian world I observed a lack of restraint in relation to war, such as even barbarous races should be ashamed of; I observed that men rush to arms for slight causes, or no cause at all, and that when arms have once been taken up there is no longer any respect for law, divine or human; it is as if, in accordance with a general decree, frenzy had openly been let loose for the committing of all crimes.

Grotius accepted that there were some circumstances in which war was justifiable and identified three 'just causes' for war: self-defence, reparation of injury, and punishment. He provided a wide variety of circumstances under which these rights of war were viable and when they were not. He also advanced the notion of what rules governed the conduct of war once it had begun. He argued that all parties to war should be bound by such rules, whether their cause was just or not.

As Hedley Bull, an Australian professor of international relations, declared, 'The idea of international society which Grotius propounded was given concrete expression in the Peace of Westphalia ...' and that Grotius was '... the intellectual father of this first general peace settlement of modern times.'

THE JUST WAR TRADITION

The philosophical and theological approaches of St Augustine, Thomas Aquinas and Hugo Grotius are outlined here as an illustration of how thinking has developed over the centuries. In fact, there were many other contributors who gave consideration to building up a convention about the morality and legitimacy of war. What emerged was the *just war tradition*, which encompassed two main categories *Jus ad bellum* or the right to go to war, and *Jus in bello* the right conduct within the war. It has now been suggested by several modern theorists that these now be joined by a third category, *Jus post bellum*, provision for conduct after a war. In the vernacular, this might be expressed as 'if you break it, you own it'.

There are various sources indicating the criteria for *Jus ad bellum*, *Jus in bello* and *Jus post bellum*; they say similar things, though with important nuances. The criteria below represent an edited collation of various authorities. It should be noted that what some people think of as the 'Laws of war' may or may not include every aspect of the three *jus*,

Saint Augustine of Hippo (354 to 430): a theologian and philosopher, he reconciled the obligation of Roman citizens to go to war for Rome when required, with a pacifist, 'turn the other cheek' viewpoint. His writings contributed much to modern thinking about legitimate and illegitimate war This magnificent depiction was painted by Claudio Coello, 1664

and vice versa. The objective here is to provide an outline. The examples quoted are selective and based on just a few cases from a vast list of current and historic wars.

FIVE PRINCIPLES OF JUS AD BELLUM: JUST CAUSE; LAST RESORT; PROPORTIONALITY; SUCCESS; PROPER AUTHORITY

JUST CAUSE
There must be a morally justifiable reason for going to war, though this may require some subjective judgement that may not accord with all parties. Justification might include maintaining the world order, self-defence or preventing genocide, but the main focus must be to establish or re-establish a just peace. That state of peace must be better than that which prevailed had the war not occurred. Wars should not be fought to acquire territory or provoke a regime change.

· *Expelling Iraq from Kuwait, the 'First Gulf War'; Operation Desert Storm, 1991 met this principle. Far from being 'all about the oil', Iraq's invasion and annexation of Kuwait was a clear transgression of international law*

LAST RESORT
This states simply that all non-violent options such as diplomatic efforts, trade sanctions or blockade must first be exhausted before the use of force can be justified. Even then, this must take into account the *just cause* criterion. Some authorities would support using small raiding parties if that would achieve a peaceful objective. Some authorities suggest that *last resort* should be abandoned if waiting until all non-violent options are tried if that would result in more human misery than otherwise.

· *On 3ʳᵈ September 1939, the United Kingdom declared war on Germany. Exhaustive diplomatic efforts in the years up to that date ('appeasement') had failed. The UK had no other choice. Hitler was determined to go to war*

PROPORTIONALITY

This principle states that the violence used in the war must be proportional to rectify harm already suffered and necessary to end the attack and to remove the threat. Thus, defeating the enemy's armed forces in the field would be proportionate; destroying cities, with the accompanying civilian deaths, would not be.

· *Following Argentina's invasion of the Falkland Islands, the United Kingdom undertook operations to recover the territory. During that conflict, the UK made it clear that it would not operate on the mainland of Argentina and confined the war to the islands themselves.*

POSSIBILITY AND PROBABILITY OF SUCCESS

There must be reasonable grounds for believing that war can achieve its objective commensurate with the *just cause* principle. Using military power for a futile cause or where there is no possibility of success would not satisfy this principle. However, we must take account of the 'honour' aspect, mentioned in Chapter 5; for the sake of national pride, it may be necessary to fight a hopeless war.

· *Prior to the British, French and Israeli invasion of Egypt to recover the Suez Canal, the UK government was advised by its own military that this could not succeed without American help. They went ahead anyway, which resulted in a complete fiasco, the UK being obliged to withdraw by American threats. The invasion failed, the UK was obliged to withdraw and the Suez Canal stayed in Egyptian hands*

Niccolò Machiavelli (1469 to 1527), often thought of as the ultimate cynic, was a clever diplomat, and astute commentator. He wrote widely on war. Not really cynical, more a realist. Portrait by Santi di Tito, c.1580

PROPER AUTHORITY

This criterion is bound up with the notion of the sovereign state, which, having a 'legitimate monopoly of organised violence', has the right to declare war, but only one that satisfies other *jus ad bellum* criteria. However, in Chapter 2, we defined war as focused on the polity, which would cover groupings other than the state, such as a widely supported rebellion, a secessionist movement or a party to a civil war. Even in this case, any organised violence would be illegal if gratuitous and would need to be sanctioned by the polity's leaders.

· *We deal with this later, under sovereignty and democracy.*

FIVE PRINCIPLES OF *JUS IN BELLO*: DISCRIMINATION; PRO-PORTIONALITY; MILITARY NECESSITY; POWS; 'NO MEANS'
Whereas *jus ad bellum* is concerned with the political aspects of declaring war, *jus in bello* directs how combatants – on both sides – conduct themselves in the course of the war.

ABOUT WAR

DISCRIMINATION

The use of organised violence should be directed at enemy combatants, not towards civilians. This includes bombing civilian areas and reprisals against civilians or prisoners of war (POWs). Soldiers are not permitted to harm enemy combatants who have surrendered or who have been captured or injured.

- *Uncomfortable as it is for the UK and U.S., the Strategic Bombing Campaign during the Second World War contravened this principle. It caused many civilian deaths and, although this is controversial, did not affect Germany's productive capacity as much as claimed.*

PROPORTIONALITY

Combatants must make sure that civilian deaths and damage to civilian property is proportionate to the military objective.

- *Although it might be morally dubious, some level of civilian deaths and casualties – known as 'collateral damage' – seems to be acceptable, but so also is the (enemy's, of course) practice of locating snipers in hospitals and schools.*

MILITARY NECESSITY

Attacks must be in line with the overall objective of defeating the enemy. The installations attacked must be a legitimate military target.

- *The US, UK, Australian and Polish invasion of Iraq in 2003 started with a two-day aerial bombardment. This was never questioned, but the scale of it and the damage it caused may have been excessive to the purpose*

FAIR TREATMENT OF PRISONERS OF WAR

Whereas it might be challenging to enforce the first three criteria because of difficulties attributing physical evidence or identifying those responsible and bringing a case, the bad treatment of POWs might rely on statement from survivors, mass graves in the case of massacres or peacekeepers' or neutral observers' testimony.

- *Generally, during the Second World War both the Germans and the Allies treated their respective POWs reasonably well. However, the German treatment of Russian POWs and vice versa was appalling, with a very small chance of survival on either side*

'NO MEANS'

The Latin expression *malum in se* means 'evil in itself', the idea being that some things are inherently evil. 'No means' is a prohibition against methods of warfare that are generally considered to be morally unacceptable, such as mass rape, forcing or inducing enemy soldiers to fight against their own side or the use of nuclear or biological weapons.

- *The most appalling example of this was the use of rape by Bosnian Serb forces of the Army of the Republika Srpska (VRS) and Serb paramilitary units during the 1992 Bosnian War against Bosniaks – Muslim Bosnians. It was part of a deliberate campaign of terror and ethnic cleansing. Between 10,000 and 50,000 women were raped*
- *Another example were the Janissaries, captured Christian boys forcibly converted to Islam and then made to fight for their captors, the Ottomans. However, this was in the fourteenth century! Modern instances are rebel groups (frequently in Africa) capturing boys and, rather than converting them to any religion, forcing them to commit atrocities to induct them into the rebel group.*

FIVE PRINCIPLES OF *JUS POST BELLUM*: RECOGNITION; POLITICAL PROCESS; TRUTH AND RECONCILIATION; CRITICAL INFRASTRUCTURE; SECURITY APPARATUS

Jus ad bellum concerns political choice. *Jus in bello* concerns the conduct of the war and thus the military. *Jus post bellum*, if recognised, is the responsibility of all parties – victors and the defeated – and also the international community. The transition from war to a sustainable peace in any circumstances is perhaps the most challenging aspect of war, particularly for the defeated belligerent. Whereas legal experts might interpret *ad* and *in* reasonably closely, *post* defies precise legal definition and is more of a political and moral judgement. *Jus post bellum* has a shorter lineage than the other two components but several themes are emerging. It should be noted that some authorities would add several other criteria to this list, so these five sets are largely illustrative.

RECOGNITION

All parties, the belligerents, dissident groups and arms suppliers must recognise that hostilities are over. A legitimate government must be established, if only on an interim basis, pending elections. There must be a peace treaty between all parties, recognised by the UN.

· *At the end of the Second World War in Europe, and although there were fears of a Nazi redoubt in southern Germany, the leaders and population accepted their defeat. There was no redoubt. The Germans were, however, resistant to Denazification, which was dropped entirely in 1951,*

ESTABLISHMENT OF A POLITICAL PROCESS

If democracy is to be established – or re-established – a healthy political process is essential, and representative political parties must be encouraged. A free but objective media is also vital. The first step in this may well be a written constitution – there are plenty of good examples of such, and also voter registration. This may mean setting up an interim system of administration to ensure that essential physical and social infrastructure is put on place.

- *After the end of the Second World War in the east (Japan surrendered in August 1945), Douglas MacArthur, as the 'American Caesar' (the title of William Manchester's biography), insisted that Japan drop the Meiji constitution (sometimes referred to as 'government by assassination') and the idea of the Emperor as a god. He instituted a constitution based on a parliamentary system that guaranteed fundamental rights. The Emperor was reduced to a symbol of the state and exercising merely a ceremonial role; the people were made sovereign.*

TRUTH AND RECONCILIATION

Most wars have instances of human rights abuses, some worse than others. Rather than letting grievances fester, such a Truth and Reconciliation Commission should be set up. Again, there are plenty of good examples to follow.

- *These are more applicable to civil wars, where Truth and Reconciliation Commissions favour restorative justice rather than retribution.*

REBUILDING CRITICAL INFRASTRUCTURE

At the very minimum, social utilities (fuel, water, sewage, transport, telecommunications) should be rebuilt, with a shared responsibility between the victor and the defeated

- *This is perhaps the most controversial aspect of post bellum. As both a negative and positive example, the original policy towards a defeated Germany in 1945 was that no help was to be given to the Germans in rebuilding their nation, save to mitigate starvation. In fact, many manufacturing plants were destroyed under orders from the occupying powers. However, recognising that a prosperous Europe required a productive Germany, President Truman rescinded this policy and West Germany actually benefited to a small extent from the Marshall Plan. Truman's successor, Eisenhower, saw Germany as the key to a peaceful and prosperous Europe.*

DEVELOPING AN ACCOUNTABLE SECURITY APPARATUS

The responsibility for security (military, police and intelligence) will rest with the newly established government, and this should be closely monitored by the international community.

· Development, *in its broadest sense, will be necessary to build up the defeated nation. The aphorism is* no peace and development without security and no security without peace and development. *It is axiomatic that this is the responsibility of the new nation. Generally, the international community is generous in giving help to support this effort.*

JUSTICE, DOCTRINES AND THE CONDUCT OF WAR

After two or more millennia of thinking about justice and war, it is useful to pause and reflect what

Prime Minister of the United Kingdom (1997 to 2007). Now reviled for his Iraq adventure (the invasion of Iraq by coalition forces, led by the US in 2001), and although British governance failed (see Chilcot), he was let down by the Americans. His 'Doctrine of the International Community', the Chicago speech, in 1999, delighted some, but many were indifferent

impact this has had on the actual conduct of war. St Augustine was writing at a time when, what would now be known as 'security threats' were egregious. Rome had, for example, abandoned Britannia in 410 because of external threats. Thomas Aquinas was writing as Genghis Khan devastating the Middle East and Asia and Grotius advanced his more secular theories during the Thirty Years' War, ostensibly a religious war but more about hegemonic ambition.

Although philosophers continued to think about war and justice during the 18th and 19th century, there is little to capture the imagination until a group of theologians and professors published a manifesto to justify actions by the German government during the early stages of the First World War. This is known as the 'Manifesto of 93'. This was a proclamation, originally titled in English *To the Civilized World* by 'Professors of Germany', declaring their support for German military action. Though it animated support for the war throughout Germany, many foreign thinkers were furious at its presumption.

The Treaty of Versailles might be thought of as based on the notion of justice (open treaties, borders, self-determination etc.) but, as far as justice is concerned, scholars are still debating whether Versailles was too hard on the Germans – they rose again in twenty years – or whether Versailles was too soft on them – they should not have been able to rise again in twenty years!

The US military, political and civil establishment were devastated by the experience of the Vietnam War and controversy still exists about the causes of the disaster. One clear outcome was that the US military, for many years afterwards, and maybe still, eschewed messy wars, counter-insurgency, peace support operations and preferred 'proper wars' against a near-peer enemy. There are still many vestiges of that left in US military and political thinking, with 'win', 'victory', 'shock and awe' very much the conventional descriptors. Nevertheless, several doctrines have emerged over the past thirty-five years to provide a guide to the use of armed force and the conduct of war.

THE WEINBERGER DOCTRINE

Caspar Weinberger was US Secretary of Defense from 1981 to 1987, under President Ronald Reagan. His doctrine was a five-point list of criteria in a speech entitled *The Uses of Military Power*. It was based, in part, on the supposed lessons from the US involvement in Vietnam, 1955 to 1975. The main points follow:

1) The United States should not commit forces to combat unless the vital national interests of the United States or its allies are involved.

2) US troops should only be committed wholeheartedly and with the clear intention of winning. Otherwise, troops should not be committed.

3) US combat troops should be committed only with clearly defined political and military objectives and with the capacity to accomplish those objectives.

4) The relationship between the objectives and the size and composition of the forces committed should be continually reassessed and adjusted if necessary.

5) US troops should not be committed to battle without a *reasonable assurance* of the support of Congress and US public opinion.

6) The commitment of US troops should be considered only as a last resort.

THE POWELL DOCTRINE

Colin Powell was US Secretary of State from 2001 to 2005, under President George W. Bush (the younger Bush, and 43ʳᵈ President of the United States). The term *Powell Doctrine* was coined in the run-up to the 1990–91 Gulf War. It was inspired by the Weinberger Doctrine, Weinberger being Powell's former superior. Powell's approach was summarised in the form of critical questions:

1) Is a vital national security interest threatened?
2) Do we have a clear attainable objective?
3) Have the risks and costs been fully and frankly analysed?
4) Have all other non-violent policy means been fully exhausted?
5) Is there a plausible exit strategy to avoid endless entanglement?
6) Have the consequences of our action been fully considered?
7) Is the action supported by the American people?
8) Do we have genuine broad international support?

Some reports convey the same meaning as the above eight points but *World Politics Review* also adds:

9) If we put combat troops into a given situation, we should do so wholeheartedly, and with the clear intention of winning. (Winning is not defined, and it is the *wholeheartedly* point that is salient.)

BLAIR DOCTRINE

Tony Blair was the British Prime Minister from 1997 to 2007. In a speech to the Chicago Economic Club in 1999 (*The Chicago Speech* is the tag), he laid out his *Doctrine of the International Community*. Like Powell's doctrine Blair's criteria subsists in the expectation of affirmative answers to a number of questions:

1) Are we sure of our case?
2) Have we exhausted all diplomatic options first?
3) Are there military operations can be 'sensibly' undertaken?
4) Are we prepared for the long term?
5) Do we have national interests involved?

SOVEREIGNTY AND DEMOCRACY

Sovereignty concerns the right of the state, having a legitimate monopoly of organised violence, to declare war. One aspect missing from Tony Blair's doctrine is that of the support of the citizens, or, in the case of the United Kingdom, subjects, present in both the Weinberger and Powell doctrines. In the case of the United Kingdom, the government has taken over the monarchical prerogative to declare war, without, it seems, much in the way of constitutional deliberation. In the US, the president may be constitutionally obliged to seek an approval from Congress to declare war, but this is more honoured in the breach. Article I, Section 8, of the Constitution clearly states that 'Congress shall have the power … to declare war', but fails to specify that it is *only* Congress that has that prerogative. For over two centuries, American presidents have assumed the right to declare war without Congressional approval. Both the US and UK systems are an affront to democratic scrutiny and control.

For example, in the US, the Gulf of Tonkin Incident led the United States into the Vietnam War. The Americans originally blamed North Vietnam, but the *Pentagon Papers* and the memoirs of Robert McNamara proved that the US government lied to justify the war.

In the UK, as outlined above, Tony Blair or his lackeys, had the dossier on Saddam Hussein's WMD 'sexed up' to oblige Parliament to back him in joining President Bush's invasion. It was approved by Parliament in a whipped vote.

THE GULF OF TONKIN

We must distinguish between the root causes of war and what occasions any particular war.

Following the end of the Second World War, the Americans became neurotic about Communist aspirations to spread their socialist vision around the world. Perhaps we should also mention that the Soviets had similar feelings about the American political model.

Witness the actions of Joe McCarthy's HUAC, the House Un-American Activities Committee, the 'Reds under the Beds' fear and the 'Better Dead Than Red' idea!

So when US ships off the coast of Vietnam thought they were being attacked, it sparked what later became known as the Vietnam War. There are many aspects to this, detailed in the addendum at the end of this chapter. This covers the Tonkin incident, the Tonkin Resolution and Operation Rolling Thunder, a senseless bombing campaign which did much to alienate the North Vietnamese and set back negotiations by years.

THE RESPONSIBILITY TO PROTECT

At the 2005 World Summit, all member states of the United Nations committed themselves to 'The Responsibility to Protect' (RTP). It addressed four exigencies: to prevent genocide; to prevent and prosecute war crimes; to deter ethnic cleansing and safeguard human rights; to further the notion that the sovereignty of a nation state commits the state to the security of its citizens, and to protect them from human rights violations. Thus, it asserts, other states have a responsibility to protect citizens of other states if they are subject to these crimes, even if this means invasion and the use of armed force. It is seen as very worthy but, according to a UN report:

'A decade after world leaders agreed on the responsibility to protect at a Headquarters world summit, the principle remained a worthy yet elusive concept, with success seen in some places, but with Syria (and they might have included Yemen as well) standing out as a glaring example of the international community's failure to put it into practice.'

CONCLUSIONS
Much of the approach to jus *ad bellum* and *jus in bello* is based on the Western, Judeo-Christian injunction about killing and 'loving thy neighbour'. Even the Romans based their approach to war on their religion and gods, though those gods might seem strange and alien to the modern mind. The *ad* and *in* of justice were terms first used to describe thinking in the Middle Ages, to be joined by the *post* in the early 21st century. However, Christian religion, is essentially not democratic, and this influences the concept of justice in two ways. First, little of the philosophical approach to war up to the mid-19th century was concerned with what the subjects or the electorates, if they existed at all, thought about an impending war. They certainly didn't get a vote on it and their representatives were largely obliged to toe the party line. War was largely undemocratic. Second, and concomitant with the first, is that the constitutional right to declare war is the most jealously guarded provision of almost all governments, be they nominal democracies, elective dictatorships or tyrant-run kleptocracies.

It was Clausewitz who emphasised the notion of 'the people' in his classic work *On War*, published by his wife in 1832 (he died in 1831). Included therein is the concept of 'the passion of the people', one aspect of Clausewitz's 'Remarkable Trinity'. The other two being *reason* and *chance*.

THE UN AS SAFEGUARD OF LEGITIMACY
The United Nations was established in 1945 with a determination to 'unite our strength to maintain international peace and security' and to 'save succeeding generations from the scourge of war, which twice in our lifetime has brought untold sorrow to mankind' and, among many other provisions, 'to ensure, by the acceptance of principles and the

institution of methods, that armed force shall not be used, save in the common interest.'

The ratification of the UN Charter in 1945 refined the principles of *jus ad bellum* and *jus in bello* into international law and also by implication, *jus post bellum*. Article 2(4) prohibits 'the threat or the use of force against the territorial integrity or political independence of any state, or in any other manner inconsistent with the purposes of the United Nations.' There are two exceptions: the Security Council may use force if it agrees it is necessary to 'maintain international peace and security' and Article 51 reserves the 'inherent right of individual or collective self-defence if an armed attack occurs against a member of the United Nations.'

Thus, the UN does not seek to limit or control war, but to prohibit it. This may have the negative effect of countries never declaring war as such, but undertaking 'pacification', 'police action' or 'humanitarian intervention' (see Libya, mentioned in Chapter 7). A moot point is pre-emptive war, where military action is taken against a likely enemy before they have started hostilities. It became part of the Bush Doctrine. Named after George W Bush, 43rd President of the United States, the doctrine also included unilateralism, attacking countries that harbour terrorists and Democratic regime change. All four aspects are anathema to the spirit of the United Nations. It is unclear whether the Obama Doctrine, if such existed in a coherent form, repudiated this.

Legitimacy, in the form of justice, legality or moral standing, will always be a contested concept. Consensus will be inhibited by realpolitik with larger, more powerful countries ignoring the concept altogether. This obviously points to the U.S. where many of its actions over the years have been legally and morally dubious. But one of the great paradoxes of war is that the world needs the United States – or at least *has* needed it – to show leadership in resolving both inter-state and intra-state (civil) wars. Perhaps that tells us more about other countries and other regional security institutions then it tells us about the United States itself.

There is much debate about whether wars are declining in frequency. On one hand there is Colin Gray's *Another Bloody Century*, on the other hand there is Steven Pinker's *The Better Angels of Our Nature*. What is not in doubt is that since 1945 the United Nations has made a major contribution to world peace and, where war has broken out, a major contribution to both resolving the issues and rebuilding post-war shattered economies. At the very least, the concepts of *jus ad bellum*, *jus in bello* and *jus post bellum* represent a framework for guidance and, should it be necessary, condemnation and the indictment of evildoers on criminal charges.

ADDENDUM TO CHAPTER EIGHT: LEGITIMATE OR ILLE-
GITIMATE WAR?

THE GULF OF TONKIN

In the early sixties, the Western world, particularly the Americans, was still wary of the hegemonic ambitions of communists, led by Soviet Russia.

By 1964, US forces were engaged in bombing supply lines to disrupt communist North Vietnamese incursions into South Vietnam and in supporting Army of the Republic of (South) Vietnam to counter raids of Viet Cong strongholds in rural areas. With US naval support, the ARVN began commando raids along the North Vietnamese coast, including coastal bombardments. On the littoral of the Gulf of Tonkin, these raids were supported by US ships nearby.

In early August, the US destroyers Maddox and Turner Joy, were on reconnaissance and engaged in intelligence-gathering patrols. In the early hours of August 2nd, the Maddox received a report that three enemy patrol boats were about to attack. Captain Herrick initially steamed out to sea to avoid confrontation, but he soon returned to the Gulf. Within hours, three North Vietnamese patrol boats were speeding towards the destroyer, and Herrick ordered his crew to fire if the boats came within 10,000 yards. They did, and one boat was destroyed, the others were damaged and retreated.

GULF OF TONKIN INCIDENT

The next day, both ships received intelligence that another attack was imminent. With visibility poor, Herrick again decided to avoid confrontation and moved both ships further out to sea. Around 9 pm, however, Maddox reported unidentified vessels in the area and over the next three hours both US ships frantically dodged what they took to be enemy torpedo attacks. Both destroyers returned fire. But a US Navy plane, flying recognisance over the confrontation claimed, 'Our destroyers were just shooting at phantom targets ... There were no enemy boats there ... There was nothing there but black water and American firepower.' Herrick himself later admitted that 'freak weather effects on radar and overeager sonarmen may have accounted for many reports.' Secretary of Defence, Robert McNamara, did not report the captain's doubts to President Johnson, however. In reviewing the ships' messages, the US Naval Communication Center in the Philippines questioned whether any second attack had occurred.

With undue haste and without waiting for further clarification, at 11.30 pm on 4 August, in a dramatic TV broadcast, the US President, Lyndon Johnson (LBJ) informed the American public of the attack and announced his intention to retaliate. He gave no hint of doubts about the 'attack'. In his address, the president assured the country: 'we still seek no wider war.' By the end of the following year, 220,000 American troops were in Vietnam.

GULF OF TONKIN RESOLUTION
On August 7, Congress passed the Gulf of Tonkin Resolution, authorising Johnson to 'take all necessary measures to repel any armed attack against the forces of the United States and to prevent further aggression.' It was the legal basis for the prosecution of the Vietnam War. But it was assumed, wrongly as it turned out, that the president would seek Congress's approval before escalating the war.

The House of Representatives passed the resolution unanimously and the Senate passed it with only two opposing votes. To be fair, Johnson hesitated over escalation. He sounded out the North, through Canadian mediation. Despite his powers under the resolution, he was willing to offer 'economic and other benefits' if the North ceased trying to overthrow the government of South Vietnam – but added that it would 'suffer the consequences' if it continued on its 'present course'. The North rejected the offer. They would rather see the war engulf 'the whole of Southeast Asia' than abandon the vision of one communist Vietnam.

OPERATION ROLLING THUNDER AND ESCALATION
Nevertheless, citing the Joint Resolution and hoping that Hanoi would capitulate under ferocious bombing, Johnson ordered Operation Rolling Thunder, the bombing campaign against the North that began on 13 February, 1965 and continued for two years.

The die was cast for the disaster and tragedy that followed. The US did not (could not?) extricate itself from Vietnam until Johnson's successor Richard Nixon's Secretary of State, Henry Kissinger, negotiated a deal with the North Vietnamese. Nearly 60,000 American men and women were killed in that faraway country, the total death toll amounting to between 2.5 and 3.5 million souls – one of the worst conflicts of the twentieth century.

9. TECHNOLOGY AND THE MILITARY-INDUSTRIAL COMPLEX

To study technology and its application to military endeavours is to enter a bewildering and, it must be admitted, enthralling world. It is easy to go further into any one of the tempting technological advances and get carried away by any of them, depending on your inclination. An entomologist might be fascinated by 'insect allies', or 'fly bots' and anyone interested in flying might be in thrilled by hypersonic glide missiles (Mach 5, no less), skipping along the upper atmosphere and hitting the target with pinpoint accuracy. Teenage boys, from their bedrooms, would marvel at cyber defence and cyber-attack protocols.

Technology, in the form of invention, innovation and application has contributed enormously to the conduct of warfare over the centuries. From the discovery of metal to make swords, particularly from bronze to steel, up to remote autonomous undersea drones, technology has dazzled military practitioners, scientists and the layman alike.

The 20th century saw the greatest technological advances in the history of mankind. Many of these were, and remain, apparent: flight, telecoms, space exploration and so forth. Many are not so obvious but just as remarkable: material science which gave us Poly-paraphenylene terephthalamide, which we know as Kevlar; carbon fibre; paint technology and automated manufacturing processes.

AN HISTORICAL PERSPECTIVE

In looking at the role of technology in modern warfare and imagining what the future might hold, it is illuminating to view the role of technology from an historical perspective. These affords us a template

Flags and trumpets used to control war on the battlefield before there were telephones and radios. Now a lot of war is controlled by computers. This may look good and useful, but it cuts decision time considerably, presenting battle commanders with new sets of problems

with which to evaluate current technology and its future application.

For example, although the ancient Egyptians made great use of chariots in warfare, there was no new technology involved in their manufacture. The Imperial Roman army was the most powerful fighting force ever, yet the Romans were no more technologically developed than any other peoples during the rapid expansion of their Republic. What they did have was superb logistics, fierce training of their troops and more disciplined battlefield tactics. The Republican Roman army lost to Hannibal at Cannae, in 216 BC through tactics, not technology. Let us look at some examples of technological advances, and draw out some criteria for evaluation.

ABOUT WAR

THE GALLIC WARS

Julius Caesar, in his self-serving book on the Gallic Wars (58 to 50 BC) mentions that although the Romans started that war with an advantage in ballistae and trebuchets, the Gauls were very quick to catch onto the idea and copy them. Any technological edge lasts only a short time.

GUNPOWDER

Generally thought to be one of the major technological innovations ever, this needs to be put into perspective. Gunpowder was invented by the Chinese in the ninth century, but only used in the West from about the 14th century onwards. At the Battle of Crécy in 1346, Edward III won against a considerably larger French army. After several unsuccessful French cavalry charges, Edward unleashed his secret weapon – six great cannons – which he had concealed among his archers. It thus won the day, but it is unlikely they took much of a toll on the French Army as each gun only fired a few rounds during the entire battle. However, the great *fire and noise*, coupled with the carnage when the ball struck, particularly on the horses, terrified the French, who retreated. The terror of new weapons may be greater than their destructive power.

Gunpowder is interesting in another way. Aside the terrifying effect of cannon, it is often assumed that the musket, powered by gunpowder and propelling a lead ball, made the longbow redundant. The full story is more involved.

A full-strength (maybe 50 kg pull weight) English war bow (not called a longbow until much later) fired an arrow weighing about 50 grams at about 70 metres per second for interest whereas the musket fired a 30-gram ball at more than 300 m/s, more than making up for the lower weight. The killing range for both weapons was about the same. The rate of fire was quite different. Whereas an experienced and trained archer could fire up to twenty arrows a minute, even the most

154

experienced and well-trained man could not load and fire a musket at more than two rounds a minute. Also, the 'Brown Bess' of British fame weighed about 4.5 kg, whereas an English longbow would not weigh much more than a kilogram – less for the archer to carry and he could thereby carry more arrows than musket *powder and shot.*

The reason the musket took over from the bow lies in the concept of the Weapons System. The traditional meaning of this has now been superseded by a modern American terminology which is largely computer-based, but the classic meaning of *Weapons System* is looking at every step between technological invention, innovation, application and general logistics. As a negative example of this, one American arms manufacturer invented a machine gun that could fire 6,000 rounds a minute. That sounds fantastic and could be very useful on the battlefield: soldiers would not have to be good marksmen, either! But then you realise that means many boxes of ammunition being carted up to the front line or carried in an aircraft on a regular basis, straining the logistics systems.

The problem was that archers needed a considerable amount of training. In mediaeval England the law said that boys from about eight onwards had to spend three hours a week (typically after church!) practising their archery. It became increasingly difficult to persuade men and boys to practise, although it is still an unrepealed English statute. In any case it takes a very strong man to pull a war bow with a pull weight of 50 kg. This is equivalent to lifting a young teenager with three fingers around a pulley at the end of an outstretched arm.

On the other hand, muskets could be manufactured in specialised factories and troops could be trained to use them more quickly and cheaply. Small wonder then that at Waterloo Wellington said that he would have found a company of mediaeval Welsh archers of great use on the battlefield: easier logistics; greater rate of fire; just as deadly. The translation from longbow to musket, based on the relatively simple technology of gunpowder, is illuminating from every aspect of innovation, application, logistics and training.

SINK THE BELGRANO!

In 1982, Argentina invaded and took possession of the British Falkland Islands in the South Atlantic. An expedition was launched to retake the islands and, during the conflict, the Argentinian ship ARA *General Belgrano* was spotted in the 200-mile exclusion zone around the islands. It was stalked by HMS *Conqueror*, a Churchill-class nuclear-powered fleet submarine. The British Prime Minister, Margaret Thatcher, ordered *Conqueror* to sink the *Belgrano*, which *Conqueror* did. The interesting point from our point of view was that *Conqueror* was armed with modern, wire-guided Mark 24 Tigerfish torpedoes, but the captain and crew found them unreliable. They therefore fired three old, unguided Mark VIII torpedoes with impact fuses and 365 kg Torpex warheads. In service since 1927, the Mark VIII was a reliable weapon for the close-range attack. (Incidentally, Margaret Thatcher's decision about the Belgrano has been controversial ever since.) Weapons systems that work in trials, may not work in the field: crews using them have to have complete confidence in them.

DRONES

It is also worth a quick description of drones, which is a term which covers very small insect-like examples, up to the American Northrop Grumman RQ-4 Global Hawk, with its 40 m wingspan, which can stay in the air for thirty-two hours. Mainly used for surveillance, it can also carry 1.3 tonnes of armaments. Tiny drones and large drones have entirely different applications; whereas some are controlled by satellite communication, a new application, some are controlled by direct radio contact, a well-known application. The main feature of drones is in the invention and application rather than the technology itself.

MANAGING TECHNOLOGY TO STRATEGIC EFFECT

So, we can see that it is not just invention that governs the usefulness of technological innovation. Caesar's competitive weapons edge lasted until the Gauls saw a ballista; gunpowder superseded the war bow partly because of the social environment and cost; seamen, particularly sub-mariners, are justifiably cautious about new technology and drones represent innovation and application rather than invention. Despite a burgeoning canon of treatises on *Drone Theory*, the large, surveillance and weapon carrying drone is no different tactically to a piloted aircraft.

Massive and continuing technological change requires the ability to conceptualise, define, manufacture or even just purchase complex weapons systems, a challenge to which the MOD seems unequal, particularly on cost control. Writing detailed industry briefs informed by strategic thinking seems to be beyond the capacity of both politicians and civil servants.

Perhaps more importantly for innovation, do those soldiers, sailors and airmen actually relate to the new technology and how it might be used? If the question seems rather cynical, recall that even ten years after the First World War and its appalling carnage, Field Marshal Sir Douglas Haig could write: '... aeroplanes and tanks ... are only accessories to the man and the horse, and I feel sure that as time goes on you will find just as much use for the horse – the well-bred horse – as you have ever done in the past ...'

Britain's new aircraft carrier, HMS *Elizabeth*, cost £3 billion to build. As a bit of a leg-pull, Vladimir Putin pointed out that it looked like one big target to him. But the joke though is on the Royal Navy: it is indeed just one big target. Modern missile technology envisages hypersonic glide missiles descending from a great height or hypersonic cruise missiles skimming along the waves to their unfortunate target. Of course, any military person will tell you that they have anti-missile protection, but

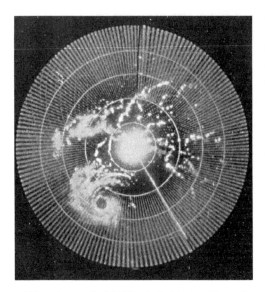

Where is everybody? Who / what is attacking us? Radar can tell you. However, modern missiles move extraordinarily fast, and it's impossible to tell what warhead they are carrying: high explosive or a nuclear device?

the enemy will not be firing just one missile. Missiles are considerably cheaper than aircraft carriers!

Let us link this to a strategic purpose. One possible threat (actually unlikely) is that Russia might attempt to infiltrate one of the Baltic states: Lithuania, Latvia or Estonia. We say *infiltrate* on the basis that this is what seems to have happened in Crimea and possibly the Donbass area of eastern Ukraine. It is unlikely that the Russians will use a massive armoured attack on these countries. Bear in mind also that Lithuania has a common border with Kaliningrad, a Russian exclave. The point is that neither the Royal Navy nor the United States Navy will send an aircraft carrier into the Baltic. No point in the Baltic is further than about 150 km from the shore, and can be easily reached with even a sub-sonic missile. In a cruel irony, even that southern part of the Baltic is opposite Kaliningrad. In particular, the Americans will not send their nuclear-powered aircraft carriers there because if one of those went down (see later commentary on *Inside the War Room*, a 2016 BBC programme), the Baltic would be radioactive for about 200 years.

Technological advance is a wonderful thing but it needs to be set against the strategic challenge. Technology to support *network-centric warfare* is essential if you are concerned about a massive Russian attack across the North German Plain, as was the fear during the Cold War. Even then, it is said that during Cold War wargaming exercises and recognising the inferiority of NATO forces versus the Soviets (largely in terms of numbers), military commanders would request politicians' permission to use tactical nuclear weapons to halt the Russian advance. Superior technology would have had no part to play. Innovation is essential but several major challenges arise in addressing some fundamental questions.

First, is the driver of technological innovation driven by the competitive strategic challenge or the desire of military leaders to acquire the very latest in terms of weapons systems? How much technological innovation is driven by a desire to keep up with the Americans? How much technological innovation, development and manufacturing is coordinated across Europe, across NATO, across the EU? Military hardware cost inflation is well known to be higher than general inflation. How much of this is due to excess profits being made by private arms manufacturers or, indeed, to the governments who allow them? How much money is diverted to consultancies and think-tanks? Why? In what areas does the MOD lack commissioning skills?

Let's take the example of QinetiQ. In 2000, the then Labour government privatised government-owned Defence Evaluation and Research Agency (DERA) and QinetiQ was set up. QinetiQ was a private limited company, which was floated on the London Stock Exchange in 2006. Hitherto, DERA had been responsible for the MOD's Engineering, science & technology, and the MOD retained the Defence Science and Technology Laboratory (Dstl) for more pure research purposes. This 'privatisation', and its relationship with defence is considered in the next section, the military–industrial complex.

QinetiQ shares were initially priced at 200p, which was generally thought to be under-priced. Sir John Chisholm, QinetiQ's chairman, bought a two percent stake in the company for £129,000 in 2002 and their value soon rose to almost £28m. It also guaranteed a fortune for Carlyle, the US private equity group that bought 34% of QinetiQ for £42m in 2002. As of April 2020, the shares were trading at about 330p. Chisholm's investment in the company showed a 17,830% return on investment, almost 180 times the initial value of the investment and one imagines a similarly generous return for Carlyle. This led to suggestions the company was undervalued. In 2008, the chairman of the House of Commons accused Chisholm of 'profiteering at the expense of the taxpayer'. In response, Chisholm stated that this was 'grossly unfair'. As *Private Eye* would comment, *that's all right, then.*

We have no particular animus against QinetiQ or Sir John Chisholm or any of his team (the chief executive at the time, Graham Love, then owned a 1.6% stake, worth £22m) but one must query whether a one third stake by an American private equity group was wise. QinetiQ must now focus on its shareholders' demand for profit and growth, rather than meeting the UK's strategic needs. Of course, they would deny this, and allude to the close relationship they have with the MOD and the military. Quite. Ultimately, we must reflect on the fact that, for all the technological capability, NATO failed in Afghanistan and Libya, the coalition failed in Iraq and no one seems able to do anything at all about Syria, Yemen, Mali, the Democratic Republic of Congo or the Central African Republic.

Technology is no guarantee, or even indicator, of success. In Afghanistan, despite all that sophistication, the Taliban, plus whatever local militia was around at the time, beat the NATO insurgency into a cocked hat. NATO lost. As a counter-insurgency campaign, Afghanistan was a resounding success for the Taliban. Despite having more troops, satellite surveillance, a more secure base, air power in abundance, sophisticated weaponry and a better command and control system, not to mention a modern PR corps, the NATO insurgency was bested by a ragtag army with little more than small arms and the ammonium nitrate that we kindly supplied them with. Referencing our *end – ways – means* model, these were simply not aligned. This is a continuous process: dynamic (in its literal sense of moving and interdependent) and contingent (depends on what the enemy is doing).

Ultimately, it comes down to what the UK needs their armed forces for. This is not a casual question. Simon Jenkins in *The Guardian* writes regularly on this subject; one suggestion is that the British Army has been transformed into an agent of peacekeeping and peace enforcement.

THE MILITARY-INDUSTRIAL COMPLEX
After the Pearl Harbor attack, the United States declared war on Japan. The Army Chief of Staff, George Catlett Marshall, one of the great but unsung heroes of the war. As *Organizer of Victory* (the subtitle of Forrest C. Pogue's book on Marshall) he led and inspired the largest military expansion, backed by industrial resources, in US history. As that time, the United States was still emerging from the several recessions that had started with the Wall Street Crash in 1929. By late 1942, only one year after the Pearl Harbor attacks, the United States was ready to enter the European war. Marshall selected General Dwight David Eisenhower to lead the Torch Landings in Morocco, Tunisia and Algeria in November 1942 against his initial preference for Lloyd Fredendall, whom he liked. Later in the war, Eisenhower became the Supreme Allied Commander of the Allied Expeditionary Force for the Normandy landings on 6th June 1944. He was not, incidentally, considered a great field general, but he had enormous skill and patience in reconciling the various factions within the Allied camp. After Eisenhower had returned to the United

States, he ran for the presidency as a Republican in 1952. He served two terms, until succeeded by John F Kennedy in 1961. For many years he was not considered one of the truly great presidents, but recently his reputation has grown. He is now thought, rightly, to be in the pantheon with Washington, Lincoln and Franklin D. Roosevelt.

It was his proud assertion that under his presidency the US *never lost a soldier or a foot of ground*. On keeping the peace in volatile times, Eisenhower commented, 'people asked how it happened – by God, it didn't just happen, I'll tell you that.' He is of interest to the US now because he knew of which he spoke, and would say: 'every gun that is made, every warship launched, every rocket fired signifies, in the final sense, a theft from those who hunger and are not fed, those who are cold and are not clothed.' He had a special disdain for arms manufacturers who took advantage of the Cold War paranoia of the day to increase their profit margins. Unless restraints were placed upon these organisations, he claimed, 'the potential for the disastrous rise of misplaced power would exist'.

Our main interest is in his farewell speech in 1961, where he used the phrase the *Military–industrial complex*, saying: 'Our toil, resources and livelihood are all involved; so is the very structure of our society. In the councils of government, we must guard against the acquisition of unwarranted influence, whether sought or unsought, by the military-industrial complex.' He went on to say: 'Only an alert and knowledgeable citizenry can compel the proper meshing of the huge industrial and military machinery of defense with our peaceful methods and goals so that security and liberty may prosper together.'

WHAT IS IT?

The military–industrial complex is described as a coalition, albeit unsanctioned, of the military and the defence industry. In the US, it is sometimes referred to as the *military–industrial–Congressional complex*, adding the US Congress to form a three-sided relationship known as an 'iron triangle'. The Americans have got rather carried away with the concept, even devising terms like the military–entertainment complex, the military–industrial–media complex, the military–digital complex, the military–Keynesianism and others. One neat arrangement, which Eisenhower might deprecate, is that defence manufacturers are spread throughout all US states, thus optimising the lobbying of senators, congressmen and defence manufacturers. This ensures that state's defence-related income, but also makes it difficult to reduce defence spending. To that extensive lobby we can add retired officers who take consultancy positions with defence manufacturers and also academics and think-tanks.

George F. Kennan was an American diplomat and historian, best known as a promoter of the containment of Soviet Russia during the Cold War. He is also famous for his 'Long Telegram' from Moscow in 1946, under the pseudonym 'Mr X'. For those interested in that era, it is worth consulting Wikipedia. In 1987, at the age of eighty-three and in seeming reappraisal of his previous position, he wrote: 'Were the Soviet Union to sink tomorrow under the waters of the ocean, the American military–industrial complex would have to remain, substantially unchanged, until some other adversary could be invented. Anything else would be an unacceptable shock to the American economy.'

Even today, the Russian Federation is seen as a major competitor, but just in case they are not, an increasingly resurgent China will serve. Other members of NATO have no choice but to follow or show disinterest.

More recently, Paul Rogers (Senior Fellow in International Security at The Oxford Research Group) has referred to the creation of a 'military – industrial academic – bureaucratic complex'. We'll resist the temptation to give that an acronym. In any case, we might add ex-ministers and MPs. In the United Kingdom, the military–industrial, maybe with the addition of 'academic – bureaucratic' complex might be referred to as 'a cosy little arrangement'. The military–industrial complex, or the military–industrial academic-bureaucratic complex is not evil or dysfunctional, just expensive, and may not quite be meeting the nation's strategic needs. Eisenhower's warning was prescient, given the United States' voiced disdain for anything that looks like state control. Actually, in reality, the US is not that much different from many other states in this regard.

A more recent example comes from Andrew Cockburn in *The London Review of Books* for February 2020, concerning hypersonic weaponry. He recognises that there was a nuclear arms race during the Cold War, with each side developing systems to counter the other is increasingly deadly initiatives. However, he says: '... if you look more closely at the history of the Cold War and its post-Soviet resurgence, you see that a very different process is at work, in which the arms lobby on each side has self-interestedly sought capital and bureaucratic advantage while enlisting its counterparts on the other side as a justification for its own ambition. In other words, they enjoy a mutually profitable partnership.'

What must be brought under control are these cosy little relationships, where the sole objective is profit, rather than the country's security. These must be replaced by tight control, strategically, contractually and cost-wise. As many situations demonstrate, the United Kingdom cannot act alone and must act in alliance with other European countries and, of course, the United States. Most of all, we need to be very clear about the strategic challenges we face, the role of the armed forces in facing them and how technology can support this. It's not simply a matter of bigger and better.

Writing in *Defence-in-Depth*, Dr Robert Foley, Head of the Defence Studies Department and Dean of Academic Studies at King's College

War Studies Department, admits that the snappily titled, *National Security Strategy and Strategic Defence and Security Review 2015* (the NSS/SDSR) was a marked improvement on the NSS and SDSR of 2010 and is a demonstration of a procedural advance the first steps of which were taken in 2010. However, he points out a section in the document: 'Innovation – generating ideas and putting them into practice to overcome challenges and exploit opportunities – drives the UK's economic strength, productivity and competitiveness.' Fair enough, but Dr Foley warns that: '... of course, technological innovation has been at the heart of revolutions throughout the history of conflict – the invention of aircraft, of tanks, of nuclear weapons all led to massive changes in how wars were conducted. Without corresponding development in the ideas about how to use these technologies, however, they would be nothing. I do not see how the United Kingdom can have a truly integrated approach to security challenges without a solid understanding of the importance of innovation and learning as the link that ties its strategy together.' There is a clear case for reform coming from this statement, and from concerns, no less acute today than in Eisenhower's time, about the military–industrial complex.

10. NUCLEAR CONSIDERATIONS

In the early morning of 6 August 1945, Captain Paul Tibbets and his crew of eleven boarded their B-29 Superfortress aircraft, which was later developed into one of the famous civilian aircraft of all time, the Boeing Stratocruiser. Taking off from Tinian in the Mariana Group, Tibbets headed north-northwest over the Pacific for six hours, unmolested by Japanese fighter planes. He arrived over the Japanese city of Hiroshima at 08:15 hours local time. From a height of 31,000 feet he dropped 'Little Boy', as it was known, the first atomic bomb to be used offensively. Forty-three seconds later the bomb detonated at a height of 2,000 feet above the city. Seconds later, 70,000–80,000 people were dead, 75,000 injured, and as many were to die over the next few months and years from radiation sickness. It was the biggest man-made explosion the world had ever experienced. In a nanosecond of atomic reaction, the world changed. Thus began the nuclear age, with its terrifying implications.

The sheer number of casualties horrifies observers, but this calculus of death needs to be put into bleak perspective. The Allied bombing of German cities killed a far greater number of people. The infamous raid on Dresden in February 1945 killed 25,000 German men, women and children. The Allied raids on Hamburg in July 1943 killed 42,000. German civilian deaths during the course of World War II amounted to between one million and 2.5 million. The American firebombing of Japanese cities from March 1945 (firebombs because most Japanese houses were made of wood) could kill tens of thousands every night. To some, it seems morally more repugnant to kill so many in an instant rather than putting in the enormous effort of thousand-bomber raids as well as risking your own servicemen. The Hiroshima and Nagasaki bombs have been described as obscene, cruel and murderous – and also illegal, as they deliberately targeted civilians.

In considering war, and particularly nuclear war, we must pause and reflect on the subject being addressed. Many people find talking about war difficult, through distaste, disinterest or not understanding what war, as a political act, is all about. Many people claim to be 'pacifists', though this may change on any rumour of war.

Many assume that anyone interested in war is something of a 'warmonger'. Students starting a postgraduate course in War Studies are asked to write an essay justifying their

The dreaded nuclear mushroom cloud. This from the Nagasaki bomb, August 1945. Although a 'small' bomb by nuclear standards, it heralded the start of the nuclear age. Nuclear weapons are a much larger, bigger bang, bigger cloud

choice, partly so that they may understand the dimensions of what is being studied and partly to weed out potential scoundrels. Many such students also find an element of hostility among their friends and colleagues; some are asked earnestly whether they had to learn to kill.

Let us recall that war is a hostile act of organised violence designed to change the political balance between polities. Yet war not only changes the political balance between polities, it creates a new political environment, both domestically and internationally. This is particularly true of nuclear war. To fully understand the conundrum of nuclear war and also the paradox of nuclear weapons (that is, how nuclear weapons have contributed to peace between the great powers), we might examine briefly the history of the nuclear-armed world.

A VERY SHORT HISTORY OF NUCLEAR WEAPONS

In 1939, Albert Einstein, who had devised the famous equation $E=MC^2$, wrote to US President Roosevelt suggesting the possibility of 'extremely powerful bombs of a new type'. In 1942, the United States established the Manhattan Project with the collaboration of British and Canadian physicists. There was concern (subsequently found to be realistic, but probably overstated) that Nazi Germany was developing its own nuclear capability. The commando raid on the Telemark heavy-water facility in Nazi-occupied Norway in 1943 illustrated this concern. The new bomb was successfully tested at Alamogordo in New Mexico on 16 July 1945 and then was used as a weapon against the Japanese cities of Hiroshima and Nagasaki.

There were also, and still are, peaceful uses of nuclear energy, but at that stage the Americans were not inclined to share their new secrets, even with the British. The British actually developed their own atomic bomb, tested for the first time in 1952, and then the first hydrogen bomb (H-Bomb) in 1957. We do not, in this book, consider the difference between atomic bomb, fusion bomb, fission bomb and an H-bomb but use the term *nuclear device*; they are all of unimaginable power.

History is full of sudden and dramatic turns, and none has had such a dramatic impact as the Cold War (1946 to 1991), the stand-off between the Soviet Union and its satellite states and the West, led by the United States of America. The development of nuclear weapons and the whole concept of nuclear strategy was, and still is, inextricably shaped by the geopolitics of the Cold War. The Soviet Union detonated its own nuclear device in 1949 and from then on it was what was subsequently called an 'arms race', with each side trying to get more effective bombs, more secure delivery methods and less vulnerable manufacturing facilities.

Nuclear devices became bigger and also smaller. The United States developed hand-launched nuclear devices for use against tank formations, and in 1961 the Soviet Union detonated a 50-megaton warhead (that's 50 million tons of TNT) obscurely called 'Kuzma's mother'. Even though this bomb was dropped from a height of 34,000 feet, and descended to its detonation height of 13,000 feet by parachute, Kuzma's mother was, literally, 'too big to be used'. Even though it was thirty miles away at the moment of detonation, the bomber dropping it was given only a 50% chance of surviving the explosion. There is now no 'standard size' for nuclear weapons, but the MIRV (Multiple Independently Targetable Re-entry Vehicle) W76 warheads on Trident have a 'yield' (the world of nuclear weapons is full of its own vocabulary) of 100 kilotons, equivalent to 100,000 tons of TNT, or about five times the yield of the Hiroshima bomb.

Were nuclear weapons a cheap (in terms of *our* casualties) way of winning any war? Or were they something that the military could use *in extremis*? Or was the devastation they would cause to the enemy, and that caused by any retaliation, simply too much to contemplate? For example, there was always concern in the West that the Soviet Union, who had more conventional forces available, would make a dash across the North German Plain and end up on the north coast and Atlantic Coast before the West could react and the Americans mobilise and cross the Atlantic. NATO high command would undertake wargames on this scenario, but most often they would eventually ask the politicians if they could 'go nuclear' to halt the Soviet advance. Of course, there were dissenters to this view, claiming that the Soviet Union had no interest in attacking the West, and there is some evidence that this might have been true. We cover this issue under the heading of *Security*.

Delivery systems are as important as the bomb itself and a range of them were developed, such as intercontinental ballistic missiles

An Intercontinental Ballistic Missile (ICBM): in silos such as these in the United States, Russia, and China (state secret, so not confirmed), these nuclear armed missiles stand ready 24 hours a day, 365 days a year to blast us all to oblivion. It doesn't do to think too much about it. There is also the continuous at-sea deterrent (CASD), with American, Russian, British, French and (maybe) Chinese submarines cruising somewhere under the ocean. Location unknown. Even then, there are nuclear armed aircraft ready to take off and deliver their cargoes (they don't say so, but they probably don't plan to return to base). This one is a Titan Rocket in Arizona

(ICBMs) and submarine-launched ballistic missiles (SLBMs). In the UK, the RAF had a Vulcan bomber standing ready at the end of runways at all times during the Cold War. The Americans continue to use this 'triad' of systems, whereas Britain and France rely entirely on SLBMs. Bombers are, of course, both more and less vulnerable to attack. On the one hand they can clearly be seen from satellite surveillance, on the other hand they can be hidden in hardened bunkers. The idea of the 'triad' of delivery mechanisms means that the enemy cannot be sure that you are totally disabled.

To clarify one point: *ballistic* means that they are only powered for a short part of their flight, and they then follow a trajectory, relying on gravity and, while in the atmosphere, air resistance. The precise accuracy of an ICBM is generally classified, but they are thought to strike within a half kilometre radius of the target. With such enormous explosive power, the accuracy may not seem important, but at one stage it was thought that a 'first strike' strategy, eliminating all the enemy's missile sites (silos) would disarm him and he would sue for peace.

But suppose a first strike was successful and the Soviet Union (the eternal enemy of choice) declared defeat: what then? There was no way that the United States could occupy the Soviet Union as Nazi Germany had occupied France between 1941 and 1944, so all that could be demanded was that the Soviets be disarmed completely. What then? In any case you cannot really occupy a substantially radioactive country. For a first strike to work, there would have to be up-to-date and accurate intelligence about where the enemy missile silos were, sufficient available operational resources, confidence that your systems had not been cyber-hacked and – maybe the biggest problem – an ability to ensure missiles could strike widely dispersed targets at more or less the same time. And, your missiles would have to strike the enemy's mobile launch vehicles, which would no doubt be disguised as trees or fire-watch towers. It is also interesting to note that, even if a mobile missile launcher was identified from satellite surveillance, by the time the missile arrived on target, the launcher could have moved. This is not something that applies to submarine-launched ballistic missiles (SLBMs), so the 'first strike' strategy was not going to work.

So nuclear strategy evolved into 'second strike' capability. This is still current policy: a country's nuclear capability 'deters' any other nuclear country's use. The catchphrase is MAD (Mutually Assured Destruction). The idea is that any enemy launching an attack on any other nuclear-powered country, would, after retaliation, not have a country left to govern. Even with the vast disparity of arsenal (see panel at end of chapter for current nuclear stockpiles), such as the few bombs held by North Korea, the calculus still works. Some American 'hawks' advocate a pre-emptive nuclear strike on North Korea to eliminate their nuclear capability. But it is known that North Korea has mobile launch sites, so could these hawks be sure that the North Koreans would not send a missile to the Bay Area on the West Coast of the United States? And even if the scenario is extremely unlikely, could any American politician risk it? This is known as deterrence. That is to say, an enemy is deterred from using nuclear weapons by the risk that the other side will retaliate in kind, leading to an all-out conflict and an extensive nuclear exchange. The vocabulary also includes *escalation*, where it is imagined that the political–military nexus can manage a controlled escalation from a minor conventional war to an all-out nuclear exchange. This ignores the fact that controlling war is extraordinarily difficult and has only rarely been achieved in history. The most recent example of 'control' was when George H.W. Bush (George Bush senior) refused to allow his military to 'push on to Baghdad' after Kuwait had been liberated during 1990 to 1991.

WHERE ARE WE NOW?
Nuclear weapons take war into a new dimension. Hitherto, the purpose, prosecution and control of war could be understood by both politicians and war leaders. They could, perhaps, draw on their own experience and certainly on the historical record. Nuclear weapons and nuclear war are different, politically and from the point of view of warfare itself. We cannot un-invent nuclear weapons. Nuclear disarmament, advocated and supported by many peace campaigners, is well-nigh impossible. The reduction in nuclear arsenals over the past thirty years has more to do with the post-Soviet 'peace dividend'

These terrifying behemoths cruise under the ocean as part of the CASD. The location is unknown, even to higher command (if this were not the case, they could be identified, and possibly eliminated, by an enemy). This is a US Columbia-class ballistic missile submarine, to enter service in 2031. These boats are phenomenally expensive; this Columbia class is reckoned to cost about $10 billion

than international treaties, although these have had an important effect. Even if a complete nuclear disarmament treaty were to be negotiated with every nuclear armed country (see panel at end of chapter), we have established that no one would have the confidence that the signatories would abide by their commitments. In any case, making a nuclear explosive device is not that complicated; it is largely a question of the enormous number of centrifuges you need to isolate the particular isotope of uranium, and then of course determine the delivery mechanism: aircraft, missile, etc.

Nuclear weapons take war into a new dimension, culturally, politically and militarily. They have spawned a whole subculture of nuclear strategists, arms control experts, lawyers and diplomats with skills in negotiating international treaties. A reserve army, ready to be called up in the event of hostilities, is now of limited value, as is the concept of conscripting civilians to fight in a war. Nuclear weapons have to be, on the one hand safe and secure and on the other ready to be used at any time and at a moment's notice, otherwise they are useless for the purposes of deterrence. This is a major challenge. This new dimension of war needs to be studied comprehensively, thoroughly and in depth, but with the core idea of avoiding it ever happening.

Whereas ballistic missiles rely on arriving at the destination by trajectory, there is a new breed of missile being developed: hypersonic cruise missiles. The cruise missile in general has been around for many years. Its main characteristic is being able to fly at low altitude while guided by various systems to arrive exactly at the destination. All weapon systems eventually find a match, and military history is littered with 'wonder weapons' that failed to live up to the promise of a winning edge and victory. At the moment, submarines are extraordinarily difficult to locate, but some self-seeking sub-sea drones may eventually find and disable a submarine. Provided there is some warning and you have enough armed anti-missile defences, cruise missiles may be countered. But the latest idea is for hypersonic cruise missiles that carry a nuclear warhead. There is some hyperbole in their advertised capabilities, but Russian/Indian collaboration and the Chinese suggest that speeds of up to Mach 5 may be anticipated, with aspirations to push this much further – possibly up to Mach 8. There is also the possibility of accurately guided missiles to descend on, for example, a large aircraft carrier from 30 km altitude. At a speed in excess of Mach 3, this would mean that it would not even need a warhead, and could destroy a carrier in one strike.

Even so, nuclear weapons maintain their potency. According

to nuclearsecrecy.com, a 100-kiloton bomb (six times bigger than Hiroshima) dropped on London would cause 130,000 deaths immediately and over 350,000 casualties, many leading to subsequent death. Blast damage would be huge – over a 10 km (six miles) circle. With the prevailing south westerly wind, the radiation effects would be felt as far away as Great Yarmouth on the Norfolk coast, 180 km away. But it is not just bigger and 'better' bombs that are, in themselves, enough to terrify anyone. There are now plans afoot to produce smaller bombs of about three kilotons, about one fifth of the size of the Hiroshima bomb. This makes the weapon even more dangerous. According to the US Union of Concerned Scientists:

... a missile carrying a lower-yield warhead like the W76-2 would look exactly the same to an adversary—it's impossible to distinguish which type of warhead it's carrying. If a US submarine launched the W76-2, a target country—such as Russia—would not be able to tell whether the incoming missile was a tactical escalation in a conventional conflict or the first move in a large-scale nuclear attack. They could easily assume the worst, and respond in force—leading to an unintended nuclear war ...

Critically, from the political point of view, and even though the W76-2 might be used in an extreme military situation (for example, taking out an enemy port facility) this 'first use' could be used by the other side, partly in fear and partly as retaliation, to launch an all-out nuclear attack with devastating consequences.

The two key arguments of this book are that war is a political act, first, last and always. Also, that to achieve peace, we must thoroughly understand war, in all its dimensions in order to prevent it. This is particularly true of nuclear war, with its appalling consequences for the human and natural world.

NUCLEAR WEAPONS PRESENT PROFOUND POLITICAL HAZARDS

There are seven main dynamics:

Accidental launch

The 2017 report by the United Nations Institute for Disarmament Research (UNIDIR), asserts that risks exist in the 'critical role in deterrence doctrine' and the 'interaction of complex systems, (and thus) the possibility of "beyond design-basis" events ...'. Concomitant with that, the 'substantial levels of investment in nuclear weapons and nuclear weapons have enhanced rather than decreased the likelihood of an intentional or inadvertent detonation event ... whereas human judgement has been key in identifying and resolving past instances of false alarms. Greater reliance on automated systems can lead to misplaced confidence, while introducing new points of vulnerability'(UNIDIR).

Terrorist groups or rogue states

There is of course the abiding concern that terrorist groups, insurgents or rogue states acquire or construct a nuclear device, but it's not just that. As UNIDIR puts it: 'technological advance suggests a declining need for terrorists or other groups to directly access an actual weapon in order to effect a nuclear detonation event.'

The sheer destruction and number of casualties, arising from even a small bomb

War is a hostile act of organised violence designed to *change the political balance between polities*. Wiping out a substantial proportion of an enemy's population and rendering vast areas of his land radioactive would not endear that population to the aggressor. One might even imagine the losing side or some of its citizens vowing to spend the rest of their lives punishing the aggressor.

Moral condemnation wreaked on whichever polity was seen as the initiator of a nuclear conflict

Although it is a terrifying prospect, a nuclear war between two nuclear armed states would probably not result in the end of the world. (The possibility of a small nuclear exchange is explored in Chapter 11 under the heading, The Future for War.) The world might even survive a nuclear exchange wiping out a country's industrial base, which would require a few dozen nuclear missiles. It is worth recording that there have been 2,056 nuclear detonations in the world since 1945.

Nuclear contamination

Contamination and fallout can and does last for years or centuries. The world is an increasingly interconnected place, and although global trade goes up and down, it generally increases. The rendering of even a small part of the oil-producing world, farmland or area where vital minerals are mined might have a devastating effect on world commodity prices. The finger of blame would inevitably be pointed at the 'warmongers'. The above hazards are well-recognised, understandable and can be made apparent to decision makers. However, the last two hazards are unknown and unknowable and represent, together, the principal overall problematic.

The difficulties of managing internal political processes

This is particularly the case with a terrified population, a political elite not having faced such a predicament before and a military keen to be seen as doing their job. In the years following the Second World War, many politicians who had served in the military became politicians. Denis Healey, Secretary of State for Defence from 1964 to 1970, served on the beach at Anzio during the January 1944 landings. Although in a more modest role, President J F Kennedy served in the Second World War. In France, Charles de Gaulle served in both the First and Second World Wars and was a prisoner of war in the First. These men generally knew what war was like, with its uncertainty, its hazards, and its misery. But even their combined experience would not have prepared them for a nuclear war, and today's career politicians could not possibly have any such experience. War is a political act and yet it has to be prosecuted by military people. Thus, the relationship between the elected politicians and the military, who expect to reach positions of great responsibility on merit, is absolutely crucial. There is little opportunity for action learning. The problems are manifold. Suppose half the Cabinet was wiped out; would a junior minister with responsibility for social housing take precedence over the Chief of Defence Staff? It is often related, with a wry smile, that the written instruction from the Prime Minister to the Captain of the submarine representing the continuous at sea deterrent (CASD) is that the Captain should listen carefully to the Radio Four *Today* programme, and if that were not broadcasting, to assume that the whole of London had been wiped out, and that he was to use his initiative in deciding whether to launch a nuclear attack. If that is true, it is the most wonderfully British 'make do and mend' scenario one could imagine. Returning to Denis Healey, he admitted very late in his life that if he had had to make the decision to launch a nuclear attack, he could not have done it.

The difficulties of managing the external (that is, against the enemy)
Political processes, particularly dogged by poor communications, can bring a lack of confidence in the authenticity of the messages being received. As if the problems of managing the internal politics were not enough to cope with, the external politics would be even more challenging. During the Cuban missile crisis of October 1962 there was serious concern that the messages the State Department and the President were receiving in Washington were not in fact coming from the Soviet leader. This was in a non-war situation. In an era of nuclear war, especially with the possibility of cyber-attacks, who would know

from whom messages were being received, even though authenticated? Who might be doing the authenticating?

NUCLEAR DETERRENCE

The UK is committed to the CASD – the continuous, at-sea, nuclear deterrent. Debate rages about whether we *need* to be a nuclear power, but several points are rarely mentioned. First, no British Prime Minister is going to forsake the nuclear deterrent while Britain has a seat on the Permanent Five of the United Nations Security Council. No British Prime Minister is going to withdraw employment from Barrow-in-Furness in Cumbria, where ballistic nuclear submarines are constructed, nor from Faslane in Scotland, their home base. Neither will they abandon this capability while France has it nor while the USA insists they keep it. Who, for example, spotted the news item in *The Guardian* for 29 July 2014, which stated: *A new agreement critical to Britain's Trident nuclear weapons system, was signed the other day by British and US officials? Whitehall was silent. We had to rely on the White House, and a message from Barack Obama to the US Congress, to tell US that the 1958 UK-US Mutual Defence Agreement (MDA) had been updated. A new amendment to the treaty will last for 10 years.* That's until 2024. Of course, the item was accompanied by a comment to the effect that *Mps also demand debate on UK's future world role,* as if they thought they might have any influence on this.

End of? Pretty much, despite the astronomical cost of replacing Trident. The latest estimate is about £40bn, with CND claiming that the true figure could be around £205bn over the life of the project and once the cost of decommissioning has been taken into account. Given the MoD's record of cost control, one cannot be confident of relying on any estimate.

Let us also dispose of one other issue: Britain's nuclear deterrent is not independent. It is inconceivable that we would launch a nuclear attack on another country without the full approval and cooperation of the United States. The only thing that might be in favour of nuclear weapons echoes Nye Bevan's 1957 comments when he said we could not 'go naked into the conference chamber', that is, without nuclear weapons. It's rather like the perennial question of disestablishing the Church or reforming the House of Lords or getting rid of the monarchy; there are very good arguments for them, but they are deeply ingrained into British culture and one would be pretty safe saying that neither will ever happen. So, is the nuclear posture a clearly thought-out policy, based on exhaustive analysis and a realistic appraisal of current and future threats and the UK's place in the world? No, it's just a default position, the renewal of unchanged decisions made incrementally over the years. It hardly amounts to a strategy, let alone a policy.

There have been relatively few technological innovations in the history of war that have changed the practice of war and hence strategic options. The first was steel swords instead of bronze. Gunpowder was not that great an innovation (Wellington's comment about Welsh archers at Waterloo). Air power, and radio communications certainly fit the bill. Drone warfare does not; there is no *strategic* difference between a drone and a piloted aircraft. Strategy is the link between politics and the use of armed force.

Nuclear weapons, however, not only changed war and warfare forever, they also changed society and politics. Although they were studied in much greater depth during the Cold War, they have not gone away; they are still potent. Scientists continue to work on them, updating and renewing them. It's an old saying, but still compelling: 'the price of security is eternal vigilance'. Never more so than with nuclear weapons.

NUCLEAR STOCKPILES OF NUCLEAR ARMED COUNTRIES

Five nuclear-weapon states under the NPT	
Country	Warheads (projected 2022)
United States	3,620
Russian Federation	3,350
United Kingdom	180
France	300
China	220
Other states declaring possession of nuclear weapons	
India	60
Pakistan	200
North Korea	7
Other states believed to possess nuclear weapons	
Israel	85

11. THE FUTURE FOR WAR

The usual approach in thinking about the future of war is to be preoccupied, even dazzled, by military technology. Stealth technology for aircraft, autonomous weapons systems, bullets that can change direction after being fired, airborne and undersea drones, missiles that reach Mach 5 and descend from 30 km, etc., etc., all inspire and terrify at the same time.

Do we contemplate the future *of* war, as a viable option for resolving political disputes, not just for us but for other states and polities? Or do we contemplate the future *for* war, having first assumed that war will be invoked at some stage and anticipating what form it might it take and how we might conduct and manage it? The dialectic is vital and can have a profound effect on the solution. Of course, we must contemplate both, and we must be clear about which. Even a cursory examination of discourses on future war reveals a fascination with the machinery of *warfare*, the practice of a military struggle, rather than *war*, a political act to gain or influence a political outcome. Civil–Military Relations (Chapter 7) hardly gets a look-in. We also need to get the balance of effort right. At the moment, UK diplomatic effort has been cut back in money terms by the same amount as we are spending on just a few new F35 fighters.

A usual assertion is that 'we live in an age of uncertainty', as if previous ages were more stable and predictable than the present, and that we are currently facing a period of discontinuities – from 9/11 to Trump, populism, nationalism, the resurgence of Russia, China, Iran – with a nod to 'post-truth', as if politicians and journalists were once models of probity. Most future war theses focus on the warfare, scaring the readers into worrying about a nuclear holocaust, mutating viruses that wipe out all but the selected few or cyber-attacks that leave them unable to access their broadband. It is war that begets warfare.

There is a significant canon of future war books and articles, some with a serious message, some written clearly for entertainment value. Some earlier works cover simply warfare, others take a more comprehensive approach, integrating war and warfare with an international relations situation. The military contribution has progressed over the years, from a Cold War perspective (Hackett), to a much more realistic exploration of some involved scenarios (Cornish, Donaldson and others). Academic contributions are complementary and accessible.

We need to examine and consider future war as part of our strategic outlook and to identify where we need to invest and configure our resources. We have a choice in terms of the mix of resources and their configurations, something that governments sometimes seem to miss. We could invest more or less money in intelligence, diplomacy, land and sea or air arms or in something usually reserved for a worst-case scenario: civil defence. In the process of doing this we will also come face-to-face with our key values, our key interests and our place in the world.

General Sir John Hackett's contribution was written some years ago at the height of the Cold War. Although that war finished some thirty years ago, Russia still serves as a bogey-man, though the Russian Federation is now more of a nuisance than a real military threat. Hackett had first-hand experience of battle in the Western Desert and during the Battle of Arnhem in 1944. His 1982 novel, *The Third World War: The Untold Story* (the update of an earlier story published in 1978 by adding more detail of Soviet deliberations) imagines an attack across the North German Plain by the Red Army. In an uncomfortable pre-echo of current concerns, Hackett imagines a Soviet Politburo, realising that the country's economy is stagnating and that its military may not be able to retain superiority over the West. They therefore decide to

The Vikings terrified Saxon England from 793 (Lindisfarne) to the late eleventh century. Fierce and fearless, they won their battles by sheer terror. In the past, Vikings raids were thought to have been prompted by acquiring gold, artefacts and slaves. Whereas this is certainly true, they eventually settled down as peaceful farmers in England. But why didn't the Saxons mount a better defence? Impossible, perhaps: the eastern sea coast of Britain is too vast. But no comfort to a peaceful Saxon, looking at his massacred family, his ruined farm and himself slowly dying in a ditch

invade Western Europe with a short, sharp blow and then sue for peace from a position of strength. They reject a sudden mass nuclear strike throughout the entire European theatre and opt for a conventional invasion with a nuclear strike as a backup option in the event of the invasion stalling. Substitute *Baltic* for *Western Europe* and you have a current, if somewhat unrealistic, fear.

NATO eventually gets its act together and the Red Army is stopped halfway across Germany. Naturally this upsets the Soviets and they launch a successful nuclear missile strike against Birmingham. The US and Royal Navies retaliate with a joint nuclear strike on Minsk, which accelerates the collapse of the Soviet effort and eventually the Soviet Union.

The book found favour with a reviewer in The *New York Times*, who suggested that it represented a 'very high order of strategic thinking' and was 'a signal to the Soviets, or even a warning of the way some Western military leaders are thinking.' Professional commentators found the book credible, and recognised that the Cold War strategic concepts were not being matched by military capabilities. Hackett understood that a defence policy should be based on deterrence and that nuclear deterrence needed conventional forces to give it credibility.

Overall, it was of its time and the high regard in which it was held reflects the thinking of the time. After the Cold War ended, there were several accounts that started: *We now know ... etc.* indicating that, although Soviet Russia had hegemonic intent, they did not seriously consider an attack of the sort that Hackett outlined. Both sides, however, made extensive preparations for such a war, a ready example of the 'security dilemma'. There was only limited coverage of the political dimension.

General Rupert Smith is a retired British Army officer and author of the supposedly seminal 2005 book *The Utility of Force: The Art of War in the Modern World*. It was widely acclaimed, some even venturing rather hyperbolically that Smith was a 'new Clausewitz'. 'War,' Smith proclaimed, 'no longer exists.' But the proclamation seems to be a literary device to catch attention rather than an assertion. He quickly qualifies this as meaning set-piece, battlefield war, what we might call 'frontal' war.

He claims that 'industrial war' was conceived by Napoleon as the *nation in arms*. He goes on to assert that, 'Nuclear weapons have rendered industrial warfare obsolete', and that, in future, wars will be 'amongst the people, with fighters part of the civilian population.' This sounds plausible, but his thinking is simply too Western or even domestically oriented. It is, indeed *our* thinking rather than that of the enemy. Smith also asserts that the enemy's objectives might be 'more political than military' as they seek to capture 'hearts and minds'. Well, yes, war is a political act, as has been asserted many times. He then advances six aspects of his 'new paradigm' of war. Such was the book's favourable reception that we reproduce them here:

1) The ends for which we fight are changing from the hard objectives that decide a political outcome to those of establishing conditions in which the outcome may be decided.
2) We fight amongst the people, not on the battlefield.
3) Our conflicts tend to be timeless, even unending.
4) We fight so as to preserve the force rather than risking all to gain the objective.
5) On each occasion new uses are found for old weapons and organisations which are the products of industrial war.
6) The sides are mostly non-state, comprising some form of multinational grouping against some non-state party or parties.

Smith's six aspects are largely self-explanatory: 1) echoes our definition about *changing the political balance between polities*; 2) 'twas ever thus; 3) strategy is never-ending; 4) are we sure that generals ever 'risked all'? 5) such is innovation; 6) covers our definition of polities. Apart from Napoleon, there is little historic perspective. The Romans, he tells us, had to contend with a lot of 'war amongst the people', what we now call 'insurgency'. Many wars since then were actually sieges. Overall, Smith's book is a useful contribution to thinking about *some* wars and about strategy in *some* circumstances. Overall, Smith's theses illustrate thinking in 2005, but he is far from being a 'new Clausewitz'.

In May 2016, General Sir Richard Shirreff, one-time Deputy Supreme Allied Commander Europe published a far less credible, though demonstrative, account: *2017: War with Russia,* and in case readers did not get the point, the strapline was *An Urgent Warning from Senior Military Command* (note: no definite or indefinite article). It is a similar scenario to Hackett's, although written thirty years later. Putin, although he is not actually named, invades Latvia and threatens to go nuclear if NATO attempts a military response. Of course, there are the usual ruses for taunting NATO: Russian special forces abducting some American soldiers; the shooting down of an American plane, etc. – all events that any half-experienced Foreign Secretary would be able to see straight through and resist. Inevitably, the whole affair reaches stalemate, neither side being willing to use nuclear weapons. The cold calculus of deterrence works again, as it had since the Cold War started.

The book ends with an illuminating conversation. 'Politicians will have learned from their lucky escape this time maybe this will improve things?' The interlocutor quickly snaps back: '... not a chance of it. There'll be lots of eye-catching, big-ticket items. Like lashing out on money for special forces or jam – tomorrow equipment ... what's needed is for the powers that be to recognise the need to put some genuine muscle back on the bones, etc., etc.' And in case the reader did not get the point: '... the unavoidable fact is that the Russians only had a go at the Baltics in the first place because their President reckoned our weakness gave him that opportunity on a plate ...'

Reviews were dismissive. Paul Robinson, on his website *Irrussianality*, in July of that year suggested that: 'Shirreff's novel claims to present a genuine near-term possibility. In truth, it is a fantasy, as there is no evidence that Putin really is a reckless psychopath, and it beggars belief that he would launch a full-scale invasion of the Baltic states out of the blue in the manner Shirreff describes.' One reviewer thought it was Shirreff who was being reckless rather than Putin.

Shirreff's novel is summarised here not because it is in any way interesting in itself, but because it may represent the way the military, and NATO in general, might be thinking. This man was Deputy Supreme Allied Commander Europe. It seems that NATO may be more interested in preserving its existence than contributing to defence. Indeed, Paul Robinson goes on to say, 'as a depiction of the warped worldview of some of the Western world's most senior military officers, it is quite enlightening.'

Shirreff's book would be edifying if it were written by a Tom Clancy or even a John le Carré, but from somebody who was Chief of Staff at (UK) Land Command and then NATO's Deputy Supreme Allied Commander Europe, it is irresponsible. In fact, the then UK Defence Secretary opined that Shirreff was guilty of 'rather disturbing conduct', and that he had made the claim 'simply to make money'. He was even obliged to deny that he had tried to get Shirreff court-martialled. NATO's existence and role are precarious enough without Deputy Supreme Allied Commanders talking up the threat; they read these books in the Kremlin too. The reaction justifies its subtitle 'An urgent warning' – just not quite in the way that its author imagines.

It is therefore with some eager anticipation that we come to *2020 World of War* by Paul Cornish, Kingsley Donaldson and others. Cornish is the Chief Strategist at City Forum and has several other roles. Kingsley Donaldson is Director of the Causeway Initiative for Peace-building and Conflict Resolution International. Both are former soldiers but they do not fall into the Shirreff trap.

The introduction covers the usual suspects: a review of the new world order since the collapse of the Soviet system, recognising that although 'security threats might not be "existential", neither will they be trivial.' With a passing deference to Hackett, they start by examining Russia's evolving strategic posture. Since the end of the Soviet area, the West has put a lot of effort into including Russia into its geostrategic considerations, including encouraging Russia to become more of a democratic, liberal, free market economy. This, the authors suggest, has failed, but they don't mention the incorporation of some of Russia's border states (their 'near abroad') into NATO. Russia's particular bugbear is Ukraine, who signed a partnership agreement with NATO in 1997 and launched talks on full membership in 2005. Those talks did not progress far and the situation deteriorated when Russia invaded

Ukrainian territory in 2014. Neither do they mention the demonstrative triumph in US circles that the western model had won over the Soviet system, which in reality fell apart because of its inherent contradictions. The underlying thesis is that *war* is about much more than *warfare*, though whatever the nomenclature, the triumph in this book is to recognise thirteen 'sectors and practices at different moments and at different levels of intensity'. Since this is the most important list in their book – and in this book – it's worth listing them. Although these are garnered from Russian activities, they raise two points for the UK and other ... let us say ... *opponents*. First, do we have the intelligence capabilities to recognise these hostile activities for what they are, and resist and counter them? Second, do we have the same capabilities ourselves? Do we need them? And if we do, are they coordinated in a strategic sense and is the location of strategic control and communication clear? Looking at Chilcot, it seems unlikely.

CORNISH, DONALDSON AND OTHERS: 13 POINTS

1) Cyber crime
2) Disruption of energy supplies
3) Preference given to Russian popular culture and language
4) Appeal to the authority of religion, ideals and ideology
5) Economic measures and countermeasures
6) Manipulative financial investments
7) Financial crime including bribes, corruption
8) Serious and organised crime
9) State-approved business practices
10) Political assassination
11) 'Cold War-style' subversion and espionage
12) Strategic communications
13) Psychological operations and deception.

These are not alternatives to the use of kinetic military force, but complementary to, and backed by it. The distinction between hard and soft power, beloved of some writers, is simply inadequate to this task and even misleading. There's nothing really novel here: each 'practice' is well understood. And that is their point: even with what we know, it is the combination and coordination of these practices that is so powerful. For example, Germany relies on Russia for thirty per cent of its energy supplies. Although Putin needs the dosh, he only needs to turn a few valves to immobilise the whole of Germany. No, it is the putative integration of all these various practices and the fact that the planning and the execution of these is under a single command. Whereas in the UK we talk (and quite a lot of it is just talk) of the Integrated Approach in an attempt to get different ministries aligned, Moscow's new National Defence Command Centre (the NDCC) has been established to organise, manage and deploy all thirteen practices. An edifying exercise is to look at the NDCC on YouTube; the futuristic theatre looks impressive but, despite every seat being occupied, it is quite obvious that nothing is actually going on. In tandem with this new doctrine, Putin is developing new weaponry for classic military power. New hypersonic missiles, such as developed in conjunction with India, the BrahMos, beat most Western missiles and it's doubtful if there is any reliable defence against them.

Well, one might say, surely the West (but let's just concentrate on the UK) can reappraise its strategic posture; refocus, reorganise and generally get the systems, processes and procedures sorted. But here is the sting in the tail from Cornish and Donaldson: 'the West has lost much of its intellectual critical mass with which to understand and rationalise nuclear and conventional strategy and deterrence and has lost too much of the physical mass of the conventional military posture without which deterrence – nuclear and conventional – lacks credibility.'

It is not what you've got, it's the way that you use it.

There follow seven regional and thematic security scenarios: *China: Unravelling Imperiums; The Afghan Factor: India and Pakistan; The Caliphate Resurrected; Arms and the Darknet; Cybersecurity; A Disunited* (UK) *Kingdom* and *Operation Perfect Storm: European Dilemma.*

The authors are at great pains to point out that the scenarios are illustrative and designed to 'underpin the central argument of the book'. They argue that instead of waiting for something nasty to come along, national strategists (whoever they are) must engage with international security as it is, and thus the scenarios are simply an analytical device. They stress that these are not attempts at prediction and they do not seek to exaggerate the situation. In fact, each individual aspect of the various scenarios is completely credible: it's the aggregation of them, the synchronicity of them, that makes them so potent. Cornish and Donaldson go on to lament the government's lack of 'broad-spectrum research and deep analysis' and identify 'the wide availability of very shallow knowledge, leading to the illusion of profound understanding'.

There is little faith in NATO either: '... in urgent need of reform and rejuvenation ... when reality proves too difficult to manage ... displacement activity such as the deployment of battle groups here and there, or the construction of new headquarters ...'. Compared with the thirteen points, NATO's position is irresponsible if not scandalous. When I asked one retired senior general to comment on NATO's strategic-political decision-making process, he threw his head back and laughed. I got the point.

The core argument of this book is that the UK government and many other Western governments, including the US, are simply not prepared strategically for any war, particularly these hybrid or non-linear wars. Neither do they appear to understand the social, political and economic factors that might contribute to winning them, as many accounts from serving officers and diplomats returning from Iraq and Afghanistan will attest.

Cornish and Donaldson's book was well received. Jonathan Powell, former Chief of Staff, 10 Downing Street, stated, 'Paul Cornish and Kingsley Donaldson are perfectly qualified to guide us through a credible and utterly convincing 20/20 vision of the year 2020, from cyber security to weapons technology, from geopolitics to undercover operations ... Knowing the unknown is the first step in making sure what we fear most doesn't happen.' The informed polemicism of this book is grounded in the authors' many years at the front line, researching and writing about security, strategy and war. They know of which they speak. As the Brexit negotiations have amply demonstrated, British politicians are still mildly surprised, and in denial, when other countries (save the Americans, who they hold in awe) manifest equal or superior skills in negotiation. War is the ultimate negotiation, be it one or a combination of the 'thirteen sectors and practices', the threat of military force, pre-emption or the use of kinetic action. The UK government, of whatever political hue, must drag itself out of the hubristic mindset of the twentieth (or even nineteenth) century and face the world as it is, and, more importantly, as it will be. Cornish and Donaldson have done the country a great service in sketching out some of the parameters but there is much more to do. They should be taken seriously – very seriously indeed.

The BBC drama *World War Three: Inside the War Room* broadcast in February 2016 developed a scenario in which Russian forces invaded a Baltic state, leading eventually to a stalemate. A US Carrier Group sails into the Baltic, only to be destroyed completely by an air burst nuclear blast, which the Russians say (inevitably) is the result of a rogue commander (who, inevitably, has been punished). There is then some argument between the British and American sides, with the unnamed US President unilaterally deciding to launch a single nuclear strike on a Russian city as payback. Although it was very well done, it was largely ignored by the critics. Maybe they missed some vital interchanges between the diplomats, civil servants and military men, some of whom played themselves. There was no better testimony to the importance of having good, informed political insights around the table.

Mary Kaldor is a professor of Global Governance at LSE and author of *New and Old Wars: Organized Violence in a Global Era* (3rd edition, 2012). Its core thesis is that old wars have been superseded by new wars. Old wars were the traditional wars of state upon state whereas new wars involve 'networks of state and non-state actors, support from the diaspora and a myriad of transnational connections, with most violence being directed against civilians.' The motivation for new wars, or maybe just the excuse, 'is identity politics and ultimately, virulent ethnic nationalism'. Kaldor is clearly distressed by this and offers, as a solution, a cosmopolitan approach, the sense of a larger human community sharing rights and obligations, tolerance and multiculturalism, civility and democracy. She obviously listens to *Thought for the Day* every morning on BBC's Radio Four, whose credo is that if everybody was nicer to each other, the world would be a better place. Though it is difficult to disagree, it does not give us very much in the way of guidance about the use of armed force.

Robert Johnson is Director of the Changing Character of War (CCW) research programme at Oxford. The central idea is that it is the character of war that changes, not its nature, which is *changing the political balance between polities*. In two brilliant articles, the first, dated 2014 *Predicting Future War*, and then, in 2017 *The Changing Character of War*, he admits that although prediction is difficult, many people extrapolate, not only from current conflicts, but from their own preferences or prejudices. For example, although it may appear that counter-terrorism or counter-insurgency (COIN) will become the normal form of war in the future, this would be a mistake. *Some* of the fighting in Afghanistan was more like First World War trench warfare. He warns against supposed paradigm shifts, such as an RMA (Revolution in Military Affairs); 'shock and awe'; 'full spectrum dominance' (there are many others), all once heralded as the key solution, and all now quietly forgotten. As Lawrence Freedman commented on the RMA, in retrospect, it looks more like a marketing exercise for more and better equipment than a serious war winner. In short, there is no predictive template for forecasting war or warfare; every conflict has its own context. We need to take care here: some of these new paradigms may just be harking back to the 'decisive battle' theory, a favourite Western trope to which some military people still adhere. This echoes the panel in Chapter 6, Strategy as the Link between Politics and the Use of Armed Force, and the examples of Waterloo, Cannae and Pharsalus. And although this might considerably upset naval historians, even the Battle of Trafalgar did not make an enormous difference to the conduct of the Napoleonic Wars. Johnson emphasises the importance of geopolitics, as covered in Chapter 4, The International Context. In terms of European security, he observes that the West cannot choose its wars. To many revisionist peoples and states observing the fattened and complacent European continent with its hopelessly inadequate decision-making processes, it is just a matter of time, resources and opportunity that will enable them to compromise Europe's security. The fallacy that the West can choose its wars has significant implications for the making of strategy and policy. Finally, Johnson comments that war is driven by 'fear, status and defined interest', an echo of Thucydides' 'fear, interest and honour'.

Peter Roberts is Director of Military Sciences at RUSI. In his rather disquieting article *Designing Conceptual Failure in Warfare, the Misguided Path of the West*, he suggests that Western militaries are constrained by 13th century theological philosophy (Thomas Aquinas,

1225 to 1274) and Napoleonic dogma. He describes the Viking raids on Britain between 793 and 850 as an important example of the relevance to the modern security dynamic. The Vikings did not possess new weapons that gave them a distinct advantage. Rather, they thought in a way that did not match the English preconceived ideas. He suggests that the central concepts of war – doctrine, strategy, approach, design, tactics – in the eastern and western traditions are not just different, they are different in philosophical terms, moral perspective and theoretical terms. He asks what are our objectives, strategies and doctrine. He supports his thesis with three strands of argument. First, that 'Western military thinking, is dominated by technology without an accompanying concept of how to employ it. There is little historic evidence that marrying information and technology, or (even) seeking greater understanding of an adversary's intentions assures victory.' Second, whereas the West sees peace and war as different ends of the spectrum, our enemies do not. Peace and war are activities that continue all the time, in harness with each other. If advantage can be gained in an otherwise peaceful situation, then so be it. The West, he implies, would agonise over, build structures and imagine a battle, and then victory. Third, western military thinking is constrained by the idea of 'battle-space', defined and delineated by time and geography. The enemies are not so constrained; they are in it for the long game, to achieve long-term interest and ultimate goals. Roberts has an intriguing argument and, like all good arguments, raises several questions. Is Roberts talking about war, *changing the political balance between polities*, or warfare, *the conduct of military affairs in the battle-space*? Judging by the text, it appears that he is talking about both, but maybe not differentiating as closely as he might. On the basis of conventional thinking, he cites Russia, China and Iran as enemies, but does not question this. One key but unasked question is how much of Russia's, China's or Iran's behaviour is down to the way they have been treated and continue to be treated – as enemies. Roberts based his RUSI article on extensive interviews with leading military observers and staff in those countries; his conclusions reinforce Cornish and Donaldson's Thirteen Points.

What, then, of the UK's place in the world? In February 2020, the Prime Minister, Boris Johnson, committed to hold the 'largest review of the UK's foreign, defence, security and development policy since the end of the Cold War. It will cover all aspects of the UK's place in the world, from the role of our diplomatic service and approach to development to the capabilities of our Armed Forces and security agencies.'

Professor Lawrence Freedman, Emeritus Professor of War Studies at King's College London, starts his rejoinder to the announcement with an article entitled *Britain Adrift* citing US Secretary of State Dean Acheson's comment in 1962 that, 'Great Britain has lost an empire and has not yet found a role.' (One wonders, incidentally, if any UK diplomat or official could make the comment that the US had lost an enemy (Soviet Russia) and has not yet found a suitable replacement – China might do.). More damningly, Freedman suggests that the search for a distinctive role continues to this day, though now in much more trying circumstances. Since the end of the Second World War, the United Kingdom has wished not only to influence how American power was applied (respected in the US but not always followed) but also to get help in sustaining its own power (not so popular in the US). A major punctuation point was in 1956 when the Suez misadventure was stopped in its tracks by the Eisenhower administration. Notwithstanding, close cooperation in the nuclear and intelligence fields continued.

How much influence then do such theses – from ex-military people, the BBC and various academics – have on the government's or indeed the military's thinking about war? It is almost impossible to tell. One can almost hear the relevant ministers (looking for promotion), the senior civil servants ('we serve the minister'), the Chief of the Defence Staff ('I do as I'm told') and the heads of each of the Army, Navy, Air Force and Marines saying they have everything under control and that, next time (whenever that is), 'lessons having been learned' and 'systems improved', the debacles that were Afghanistan, Iraq, Libya won't happen again. But you don't have to be a cynic, just slightly sceptical to question this. Perhaps the policy is that the Armed Forces will not bother with these sorts of engagements at all, with a preference for following the American line of fighting 'proper wars'. In the Strategic Review for 2015, for example, counter-insurgency, a major preoccupation of the previous fifteen years and more, seems to have disappeared. The British Army has considerable amount of knowledge and experience of counter-insurgency, some, though not all, of which is thoroughly justified based on their experience in the Malayan Emergency (1948 to 1960) and in the 'Troubles' in Northern Ireland (1969 to 1997). Despite hundreds of PhDs completed during that time, it is now – what ... redundant? Do we focus on high-end war-fighting but not counter-insurgency, peacekeeping or simply low-key military activities? But, most of all, how do we cope with the threat from Kaldor's New Wars, or Cornish and Donaldson's Thirteen Points. And if Robert Johnson's observations are correct in any way, it is a long journey from the usual results of any strategic review.

Freedman's percipient comments about the UK's place in the world must be the start point for any consideration of what sort of capabilities we need, how they should be configured and what governance should be put in place for managing conflict. Most worrying though are Roberts' deductions from his research interviews. The subtitle of his article, *The Misguided Path of the West*, indicates not only the 'same old' approach to military configuration, but also an egregious unwillingness to integrate political thinking into the direction and use of military force.

12. RECONCILING THE NARRATIVES

War is a paradox: modern, supposedly sophisticated states using controlled violence against similarly endowed polities; men, and increasingly women, being asked to fight, to kill and to destroy and then return to a peaceful civilian life; political leaders preaching peace yet, inevitably, preparing for war with considerably more effort and investment in the latter than the former.

The primary duty of a modern state is the security of its citizens.

Despite avowals of seeking peace, governments spend considerably more on war than on peace

Physical security in the first instance, with many other supporting aspects. Defence is therefore the most important task of any government. War has no origin other than human agency and it is human agency that can control, ameliorate, manage and maybe even eliminate war.

At an introductory level, this book has covered a wide range of subjects. The subject matter of any one of the chapters could support a library of books, papers and PhDs. It has laid out one dozen aspects of modern war, each signifying an implicit question such as *why does the UK not do strategy?* The book has not attempted to answer these questions, but to put the reader in a better position to ask the questions and appraise the answers, if such come.

History is about both continuity and change and I have tried to link ancient wisdom with a modern perspective. Robert Johnson's *fear, status and defined interest*, is a direct echo of Thucydides' *fear, interest and honour*. The Romans, Charlemagne and Napoleon all had similar strategic and geostrategic problems to those we have today. What we now call the Middle East was troublesome even before the Romans, who had to deal with several Jewish revolts, as had Alexander the Great before them. Stepping back from the immediate, I have been struck by several hiatuses in the narrative.

The first is a lack of commentary about adversaries – other states or polities – in the general discourse, from the MOD, the FCO and many academics and think-tanks. What adversaries, one might ask? Well, that's the point: not *who* we might see as adversary states or polities, but the *nature* of the adversary. The adversary might be skilled political dictators, rabble rousers, rebel leaders, warlords, insurgents or secessionist factions. Recall that the American Civil War was fought to prevent the secession of the southern states from the Union, rather than to end slavery. AJP Taylor's verdict on the Second World War was that both the United States and Soviet Russia just 'wanted to be left alone', the same answer from the people in FATA. It is also about *what* we might see as an adversary. The Cornish and Donaldson book, together with Peter Roberts' paper, suggest such radically different approaches to thinking about adversaries, of which there is very little in the various strategic reviews.

The second gap is between the knowledge and experience of commentators like Rupert Smith, a fighting general and Peter Roberts, an experienced academic and the way that the armed forces are configured and resourced. How, for example, do we decide to spend resources on arms rather than intelligence?

The third gap is how we in the UK, think about war. The United Kingdom is often accused, quite a lot by its own citizenry, of nostalgia for Imperial glory. That may be partially true, but it is more likely that citizens, politicians and even military people see 'war' through the prism of the First and the Second World Wars, even if they were not alive at the time. These were global conflicts involving the whole nation, supported by an extensive empire. They were *frontal* wars; once the enemy – Germany or Japan – was *pushed back* and territory *liberated*, *victory* could be assured. But each of those terms in italics may not have any meaning in today's world. How do you push back the urban guerrilla who hides among the population? How do you achieve victory? As Rupert Smith suggests, war could be never ending.

The fourth gap is what we might call 'lower-level' military activities. People have struggled with defining this exactly, but it is all those other things that militaries do which are not exactly war-fighting. During the colonial period, this was known as *Imperial Policing* (the title of a seminal book by Charles W. Gwynn, 1870–1963, a major general in the British Army, a geographer and writer). We now have *Peacekeeping* and *Peace Enforcement* (collectively known as *Peace Support Operations*), *Counter-Insurgency*, humanitarian aid and state-building. The British

ABOUT WAR

Armed Forces – or largely the Army – have been doing this for centuries. The Malayan Emergency of 1948 to 1962 is the best known, as is the Army's deployment to Northern Ireland during 'the Troubles' of 1967 to 1998; both were successful. Strangely, though, *Counter-insurgency* has disappeared completely from strategic reviews. Do we have no further interest in this? Indeed, what about 'Liberal Interventionism'? If called upon, either as part of a coalition or on our own, to help free an oppressed people from an aggressive invader or a genocidal tyrant, do we politely refuse or has all the effort gone into massive aircraft carriers and exotic aircraft? Whatever the answer, it should be made clear; the specification of equipment, the type of training and the organisation are all dependent on the role the armed forces will be called upon to play.

But the fifth, and most egregious gap is the relationship between politicians and the military and in the formulation and execution of strategy. The concept of 'Grand Strategic Narratives' sometimes raises its head but, since strategy is situation-specific, they have little utility. The 'Global Britain', beloved of Theresa May was worse than a chimera, more of an embarrassment. Even though Britain's military spend is probably the fifth largest in the world, much of this is wasted and we simply do not have the resources to assume any sort of global role. That gap is also explicit in that strategic practitioners might be ignorant of the full dimensions of its meaning, though it is difficult to identify who these people might be in the first place.

On a more practical level, some of the comments coming out of the Chilcot Report (Chapter 7, Civil–Military Relations and Governance) are simply confounding ... *grand strategy* (policy) *and strategy passed as ships in the night* ... or ... *did we develop a strategy* (systems, processes, procedures) *for engagement with the US* ... and leave the reader reeling. The 'Search me, guv,' comment from General Mike Jackson is simply incredible.

Yet the UK government, overall, is in denial. Being one of nine nuclear powers (including Israel, who does not admit to having nuclear weapons) and being one of the five permanent members of the United Nations Security Council creates the illusion that it has a major position and considerable influence in the world.

Yet it is a chimera: Britain's military/political capability is not commensurate with these blessings. In fact, in short, many commentators say that Britain punches way below its weight, not above it. The reasons for this are manifold. Some would claim the lack of any independent foreign policy since the Suez fiasco in 1956, or that the MOD is ridiculed in Whitehall for inefficient procurement. And despite efforts to sponsor an 'Integrated Approach', Whitehall departments don't really work well together, and neither do their respective ministers. The United Kingdom has inappropriate military equipment (armour, ships, aircraft) for the tasks it imagines it will be presented with, and, even more disturbingly, it is way too far behind in missile technology. The armed forces may not even be able to defend the British Isles themselves.

The American experience is different but just as dysfunctional. The United States has an enormous military resource and also a worldwide intelligence and diplomatic apparatus. Their problems are twofold.

First, there are differences in outlook between their military, manifest in the Pentagon, and their ministry of foreign affairs: the State Department. Two illustrations will suffice. Prior to the invasion of Iraq in 2003, the Pentagon and 'State' hardly had any constructive dialogue about the invasion or about post-invasion plans. At one point after the invasion, the military commander Ricardo Sanchez refused to share his military plans with Paul Bremer who, in theory, was the Presidential Envoy to Iraq. What astonishes any observer is that this could happen to a supposedly mature democracy with such enormous resources at its disposal.

The United States' second problem is simply summed up in the old aphorism, 'if all you've got is a hammer, then every problem looks like a nail', variously attributed to Abraham Maslow and several other sources. We might illustrate this by quoting a couple of headlines in the US journal *Foreign Affairs* in 2020, such as *The Over-militarization of American Foreign Policy* by Robert M. Gates, a former US Secretary of State for Defense, or, even more eye-opening, *America's Opportunity in the Middle East: Diplomacy Could Succeed Where Military Force Has Failed* by Daniel Benaim and Jake Sullivan. Who knew? What, one might ask, were they doing before?

Some wars are necessary; most are not. AJP Taylor, mentioned above, is sometimes dismissed as a 'popular historian', a mildly damning verdict that supposedly 'professional historians' often offer. Of 19th-century wars, he perceptively remarked that 'Bismarck fought "necessary wars" and killed thousands: the idealists of the twentieth century fight "just" wars and kill millions.' Defining *necessary wars* might lead us into elaborate political and philosophical arguments, and even then fail to reach any consensus. But war may be necessary to counter an actual or potential invader or anyone who seriously threatens a polity's security with military power. Even then, and because war is so costly, the case for war has to be very clear, and diplomatic efforts exhausted. Once war is invoked, the 'war vector' then continues, with each step manifest in the sequential chapters of this book.

It is often claimed that the world is an 'increasingly dangerous place', but it always was, and probably always will be. Human agency can change that, but first we have to have a response to the implied questions in this book: *What is war? What causes war? How do we stop or at least manage war?*

We began with the observation that war has no origin. But it can have a destination: peace, security and prosperity for all. But only if we retain a sense of perspective, particularly about the utility of war, which may, except in exceptional circumstances, be considerably less than was anticipated before hostilities began.

Rather than entering into literary contortions of crafting a neat, all-purpose but ultimately disingenuous answer to the core questions about war, let us end instead with an exhortation, based on Churchill's famous dictum: 'In war, resolution; in defeat, defiance; in victory, magnanimity; in peace, goodwill.' All wars should be about the subsequent peace, about a better and more mutually beneficial relationship between states or polities.

This may be about safeguarding an agreed International System or enforcing mutually agreed treaties. Punitive wars, proxy wars, wars of conquest and wars where the protagonists are not sure of their case should be considered by the international community as morally dubious. Diplomats, some politicians, NGOs and lobby groups put an enormous amount of effort and money into defining, encouraging and promoting peace. The development of human rights, economic development and trade all play their part. But whatever amount of effort and money go into peace, this is completely dwarfed by the effort and resources put into war. Let us also hope that the same, if not more, effort might go into the definition and reinforcement of peace or, more importantly, peace and security. Peace will never be understood, let alone achieved, if war, its causes, progress and conclusion are not fully comprehended by all participants before any decision to go to war is made.

According to the World Economic Forum, the world continues to 'spend vastly disproportionate resources on creating and containing violence compared to what it spends on peace. For example, in 2015 (the latest years for which figures are available), UN peacekeeping expenditures of $8.27 billion totalled only 1.1% of the estimated $742 billion of economic losses from armed conflict.' When looking at peace-building, activities that aim to create peace in the long term, these totalled $6.8 billion – or only 0.9% of the economic losses from conflict.

To convey what one needs to know about war may have been an ambitious objective, but it is only by understanding war in all its dimensions that a lasting peace – for all – can be achieved.

FURTHER READING

There have been many references in this book to various academics, military officers and think-tankers. Any list of those books, papers and reports consulted would be too much to digest, so I offer here some authors, any of whose writings are worth reading:

Sir Michael Howard (1922 to 2019), founder of the Department of War Studies, King's College London and co-founder of the International Institute for Strategic Studies (IISS) with Sir Lawrence Freedman;

Sir Lawrence Freedman, Emeritus Professor of War Studies at King's College London and a member of the Iraq Inquiry;

Professor Colin Gray (1943 to 2020), Professor of International Relations and Strategic Studies at the University of Reading;

Professor Eliot Cohen, an American political scientist and Dean of the Paul H. Nitze School of Advanced International Studies;

Professor Paul Cornish, Visiting Professor, LSE IDEAS, London School of Economics, and Professorial Fellow, Australian National University;

Professor Andrew Dorman, Professor of International Security at King's College London;

Dr Robert Johnson, Director, Changing Character of War Programme, Faculty of History and Fellow of Pembroke College, Oxford;

Professor Malcolm Chalmers, Deputy Director-General of the Royal United Services Institute (RUSI);

Professor Peter Roberts, Director Military Sciences, Royal United Services Institute (RUSI).

INDEX

Some words, such as 'Strategy' appear many times in this text. This short index is intended to identify just the main references.

CHRISTOPHER K PIKE

Author, essayist and alumnus of the Department of War Studies, King's College, London. Christopher Kenneth Pike was educated at St Clement Danes Grammar School in London and holds a Master's degree in Business Administration (MBA) from Manchester Business School and a Master's in War Studies from King's College, London. A career in business strategy, teaching and practising led to an interest in military history and strategy in general, and he writes regularly on these subjects. He was elected to Council of the Society for Army Historical Research. He lives in London and Norfolk and is a frequent visitor to the battlefields of Europe, seeing the lie of the land and the 'Other Side of the Hill' for himself.